How To Get A Job In 30 Days Or Less!

Discover Insider Hiring Secrets On
Applying & Interviewing For Any Job
And Job Getting Tips & Strategies To
Find The Job You Desire

By

George Egbuonu (M.B.A.)

Publisher: Helping Feet

Visit us on the web:

www.HelpingFeet.com
E-Mail: info@helpingfeet.com

Thank you for purchasing my book. Please take a minute to *REVIEW* this book on Amazon when you are done reading it.

I need your feedback to make the next version even better.

Thank you so much!

Contents

"Register now for a FREE online WEBINAR on

How To Get A Job In 30 Days Or Less!

and receive a FREE Special Report on

7 Great Jobs That Are Always Hiring

www.helpingfeet.com/webinar

INTRODUCTION

If you're reading this, chances are you're a skilled, motivated and hard-working individual who has come up against the seemingly unshakable obstacles our current economy has presented. But this is the beginning of a new phase in your career. Not only will you regain your financial equilibrium and ability to survive, you will see changes in your professional life that will allow you to finally thrive. Using the methods and principles you will discover in this book, you will be able to get a new job in 30 days or less. Get ready for a journey that will be illuminating, instructional, and even fun. Regardless of your work history or past experiences, everyone reading this will discover some fantastic tools to get the job you truly desire.

Anyone that has been fired/laid off or lost their job or is just trying to get a new job in today's economy has likely had a very difficult time getting a new job. This is probably because no one has taken the time to instruct you on how to get a job in this current economy.

The simpler adages on job hunting no longer apply and often times the well-meaning advice one receives can be dated and outmoded. What winds up happening is that many applicants use the same old methods for the very few jobs that are available. This is the equivalent of standing in a crowd waving a red flag identical to everyone else yet somehow expecting to stand out. When everyone is applying for a job the same way, you're better off doing it differently. In this book, you will discover job getting secrets. I will share with you precisely what new and different methods will help you move forward.

The secrets I'm going to share with you will work for you regardless of your level of education or lack thereof. They will work for you if you have no degrees, a high school degree, college degree or PhD. They will even work for people of any technical ability as long as you apply my teachings diligently. Truly, the techniques I will outline for you are totally foolproof and will not play favorites. They will work for people of all ages, races, colors, genders, or religions. Even if you've come to believe you're lacking in charisma or attractiveness or have some other long-held belief that you believe is an obstacle to your employment, those perceived disadvantages are all irrelevant.

The methods you learn here will allow you to obtain not just another job to keep you afloat but a job that you truly desire and are passionate about. You will find the job of your dreams, one that makes you look forward to going to work when you wake up. So say goodbye to dead end jobs!

The technique I teach will not require an endless amount of time or energy. All that is required from you is to try something different.

You're probably wondering who I am, so I'll give you a quick background about me. My name is George Egbuonu. For those who don't know me, I have been fanatically studying how people get jobs. This passion – or obsession, as my friends would say – began when I applied for and received my first job with just a high school diploma. This may seem unremarkable, except when you realize that this happened in an area where the unemployment rate was *seventy percent*. (That's right: not seventeen, SEVEN ZERO!) I have been able to stay continually employed in new careers, after obtaining my Mechanical Engineering degree and later getting an advanced Masters in Business degree, or an M.B.A. in the USA.

I grew up in Africa, where I spent my teenaged years, before moving to the United States, where I still reside today. In Africa, the unemployment rate hovers somewhere around 70%. I remember thinking when I was still in high school, "what's the use of studying when there's little to no hope of getting a job?" With such a high unemployment rate, you couldn't really fault me for thinking in such a way.

But one day I remember sitting in traffic on my way to school and seeing all these people on their way to work. I thought, "How are these people working? How did they get their jobs in such adverse circumstances? What is the secret to getting a job when so many people can't?" You see, I really didn't have any choice. I had to figure out a way to approach this problem as a matter of sheer survival. This incident was the birth of my need to study and understand this pattern, or even discover if there even was a pattern. My resources were extremely limited but I was driven to discover any information I could. I started out by using my pen pal network to send me books or magazine articles.

Some of you reading this are probably too young to know what a Pen Pal is. In the days before the global availability of the internet, it was a system that paired together young students from various countries around the world and put them in contact with each other. The students would exchange letters the old-fashioned way, via "snail mail," and in some cases eventually speak on the phone. Just like Facebook and Twitter today, being a pen pal was heavily popular among young people in the 1980s and early 90s. Through the aid of my international network of friends, I was able to get books, tapes and all sorts of information to facilitate my search. I eventually was able to contact hiring managers, human resources professionals, recruiters, and any types of professionals who were knowledgeable in the science of getting a job. My network grew even wider and I was eventually able to contact experts all over the world, including the United States, and was imparted with the wisdom of CEOs, business owners and entrepreneurs.

The expertise I accumulated enabled me to get my first job, even with the ridiculously oppressive unemployment levels

I've mentioned. Even though I'd received a wide range of expertise from all the individuals who were so gracious in letting me know their methods, I was still unsure what the specific parts of their instruction had actually been the deciding factor in getting me a job. I knew so much, but without understanding what exactly the secret was of getting my job.

A few years later, I relocated to the United States. Using the secrets I'd learned, I was able to get a job right away, even without any American educational history or work experience. I got a high paying job with benefits and even a signing bonus by using the secrets I talk about here. So it was undeniable that this information I had transcended geography. I was able to use my inside edge to get a job in 70% unemployment in Africa and in the US, where the unemployment in my state at the time was around 9%. It became undeniable that I was on to something when I shared my experience and expertise with my friends, who also had limiting factors in their job searches, and they were each able to get a new job almost instantaneously. After my friends got such fantastic results, they started talking about me to their friends, almost all of whom immediately sought me out for help with their job hunts. I was in a surprising situation of being quickly sought after as a career coach by people who needed help finding a job. I began coaching people one on one, which led to me sharing my information with people through formal courses and through formal video and web-based training.

During the dot com recession in 2001, I held training sessions for newly laid off workers. Without fail, every single person who attended my training sessions got a new job. It took some longer than others, but they were all gainfully employed within a short time. With the major recession which started in 2007 and current ones, I have received innumerable requests for my services both locally and overseas. This recession has affected people in every walk of life and socioeconomic strata, and accordingly, I have coached everyone from high-level CEOs to displaced minimum wage earners. I have been grateful to be in a position to help so many people, whether it be one-on-one, at a seminar, or via a radio or television appearance. I have offered my services free of charge to those who were desperately in need. I have also charged thousands of dollars to help people whose need was great, but were still able to pay for my services as an investment that would repay them many times over. What most excites me isn't simply helping people get a job. It's helping people get the job of their dreams. There is something so incredibly satisfying about seeing someone's life and entire person become revitalized through a job that ignites them.

The reason so many millions of people are unable to get a job is for the most basic of reasons: **no one ever taught them how**. There is a glut of misleading and distorted information out there being served up to job hunters every day. Unfortunately, job hunters are in a situation where they will often accept opinions as facts when it comes to finessing what feels like an impossible situation. Once he or she gets an interview, it becomes a nerve-wracking situation where every resumé must be perfect and the applicant has to say and do everything correctly. Unfortunately, during the interview process, many people in the hiring position are looking for an undefined ideal. This manifests itself with unrealistic expectations, where an interviewee is being judged harshly and penalized for any minor mistake, or for simply not being exactly what they had envisioned. The person hiring you, or not hiring you as is more likely the case, isn't interested in factoring in an applicant's nervousness or anxiety that may have affected their interview performance. They simply don't care when they have so many people begging, sometimes literally, for the same job you're after. In fact, some employers even mention in their ads that only the currently employed may apply. It's unfathomable, yet a harsh reality.

But enough with the bad news. You, sitting right where you are now, reading this, are at the beginning of a vibrant and powerful career transition. No matter how depleted or pessimistic you may feel, it doesn't matter. This isn't just a book; it's a toolbox. I use this metaphor because it doesn't matter whether a handyman is optimistic or discouraged: his hammer will still work the same. Let's get started building your new future.

GETTING STARTED

No matter how intelligent you are, or how many other books on this subject you've read, I bet you're making three mistakes common to all job seekers. Regardless of your diligence, work ethic, marketability, and intelligence, I've seen these mistakes played out again and again by almost everyone I've coached.

But before we discuss the mistakes, we need to clarify what a job really is. Yes, I'm serious, and no, I'm not being patronizing. Through my conversations with thousands of unemployed people, I've come to see that this is an incredibly loaded three-letter word that we can break down to a simple definition. A job is simply you selling your time for money. You agree to work a certain number of hours per day – generally 8 – for a specific dollar amount per hour. Or, if you are a salaried employee, for "x" amount per month. For example, you agree to work eight hours a day, Monday through Friday, for twenty dollars an hour or $3,200 per month. It's that simple. Just as a merchant sells goods or services, you're selling your time for money.

Now that we've defined what a job actually is, let's uncover the three most common mistakes a job seeker makes. Once you learn what these mistakes are, you'll regain the courage and confidence to be hired for any job you desire. You'll also experience a lot less stress and internal resistance in the process of seeking the job you deserve. This new awareness will cause any lingering anger you have about being fired or laid off to dissipate in the process.

So let's delve into what you're doing that is probably obstructing your path to prosperity.

3 Mistakes Job Seekers Make

Lack of Preparedness

The number one mistake I find in job seekers across the board is a lack of preparedness. This can manifest as having a mediocre resume or cover letter; showing up to an interview unprepared; or preparing too little or not at all for interviews. An astounding number of job seekers go into an interview knowing next to nothing about the company they're interviewing with.

I had an experience in which I coached a client before his interview, giving him information I was personally privy to about the company he'd be interviewing with. Baffling, he didn't read any of the information I'd prepared. When he showed up to his interview and was asked what he knew about the company, he said, "absolutely nothing." On top of this insult to the company, it reflected an individual who was willing to work someplace he knew absolutely nothing about. In romantic relationships, the equivalent to that would be marrying a complete stranger. If you think this analogy is too extreme, remind yourself of how much time you spend at work as opposed to how much time you spend with your spouse. In most instances, you see your spouse less than your coworkers.

So if you're seeking a job, one of the most important foundations is to research the company you're interviewing with, know the people that work there, and be able to discuss some of the key issues facing their industry, as well as professional trends and their competitors. It's also important to have a plan for your first 90 days in the job and be ready to discuss it. Right away you'll stand apart from the other interviewees who have not demonstrated their understanding of the company.

Another point that falls under the category of lack of preparedness is not being dressed appropriately or being distracted during an interview. In the electronic age, it is of utmost importance to turn your cell phone off completely before an interview. In the event that you've forgotten to do so and it rings during a meeting, promptly turn it off. Never - I repeat – *never* answer your phone during a job interview. Nothing will tell an interviewer you don't respect her, her company, or her time more clearly than this one action. As long as I'm establishing the very basics, I'll add these requirements: no smoking, chewing gum, or drinking anything besides water during an interview.

Having weak communication skills is another byproduct of lack of preparedness. Let me share a secret with you: effective communication during an interview simply means being enthusiastic about the job. When you are enthusiastic, you communicate better.

Focus on what they want and not what they have to offer the company

The second mistake job seekers make is that they become so focused on what they want, that they neglect to focus on what they have to offer the company. Many applicants fumble on this vital step. When you go in to an interview, you need to drive home the narrative that your skills, abilities, education, and personality fit the company's needs perfectly. If you can persuade them that you are able to do this job for them effectively, it will go a long way to giving them the peace of mind they need to hire you.

Negative Attitude

The third mistake is having a self-defeating, negative attitude. A bad attitude is by the far the worst handicap one can have. In the course of a long job search, it's only human to get tired, discouraged, and to feel like you will never find a job. There can also be anger or resentment one feels at having been fired or laid off.

Ask yourself these questions: Did you hate your last job? Was your last boss a jerk? If so, keep it to yourself. Or at least, to yourself, your friends and family. Despite the challenges you're facing, it's important to stay positive when communicating with networking contacts, recruiters and hiring managers. Nobody likes a complainer, even if your complaints are legitimate. Never bad-mouth a current employer, a former employer, any past or present co-workers, or even your competitors. It will make people too uncomfortable to help you, and even if they agree with you, it will make you seem tactless and potentially difficult. So regardless of what's transpired, make it a priority to come across as a positive person in your interviews and in all your professional interactions.

Above all else, remind yourself that you are hirable. You've worked before and you'll work again. Or if you're brand new to the job market, you still possess strengths and talents that someone will pay you for, regardless of how long you've been looking. If you feel discouraged and need to "psych yourself up" before an interview, do it. Whatever process works for you to feel that you can walk into a room and show your desirability to a potential employer, embrace it. This can even be a fun process where you play your favorite song on the way to your interview. Or it can be something that you know will clear your head, like talking to a trusted friend or going for a walk someplace that's special to you.

But wherever you see yourself with regards to these three mistakes, it's absolutely vital that you change this behavior. As long as you're doing these things, you will stay stuck, battling the same limitations that have been holding you back from a more enriching path.

Once you're able to turn over a new leaf, you're on the road to getting the job that you desire.

How People Get a Job

This diagram reflects how most people go about getting a job.

In every instance, a job hunter begins with the straightforward goal of getting a job. Having set this goal very easily, they take action. If they are rejected, they go back to the second step: "Take Action." But because they are still making the same mistakes, when they take the same action again, they revisit the same rejection. This continues again and again, with the job seeker's enthusiasm being depleted again and again. This is what most people do, and this is how most people apply for jobs.

Instead, your process should resemble this:

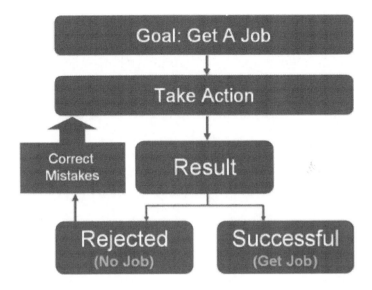

Once you've had the experience of being rejected, it's time to evaluate and hone your process to eliminate any mistakes. These changes will positively affect how you are perceived by prospective employers and will lead you to the box on the bottom right: "Successful!" While some may balk at the oversimplification of this chart, it's simple out of necessity. Millions of people are repeating the same actions that are forcing them to remain out of work, and without any changes in their actions, that's how things will stay.

3 Key Steps To Get A Job

Now that we've focused on eliminating the habits that are holding job seekers back, it's time to help by introducing some actions that will galvanize your job search and lead you to your new job. Remember, a job is simply you selling your time for money.

First, your communications with any prospective employer – whether it's a phone call, an email, or a job interview – must incorporate these three messages:

1. **Here's what I've got.**

2. **Here's what I will do for you.**

3. **Here is what I want you to do next for me.**

This will give the hiring manager or whomever you speak to the most persuasive information possible in deciding whether to hire you or not. I know it sounds extremely simple, but there is an art and a science to effectively offering your time for money. Let's discuss what exactly I mean with each of these bullet points.

Here's What I've Got

Here you'll notice that I didn't say, "Here's what I know." Your employer doesn't care about what you know. In fact, it has little relevance to your employer. It's what you can do with what you know that really counts. Nothing else matters, but this is where the majority of people go wrong. They believe that because they have some specialized knowledge of some sort, that they should be employed. Or they may think that a certain degree, qualification, or number of years of experience is sufficient enough to get them a job. Others believe that the severity of their need will lead to someone taking pity on them and giving them a job. This, again, is one of the main reasons why so many people have a hard time getting a job. In the midst of all these ideas about why they should be hired, they omit the reasons they are valuable to prospective employers.

Here's What I Will Do For You

This is the step where you demonstrate your enthusiasm for the position, whether it's in your meeting, phone conversation or in your well-crafted cover letter and resume. Your positive attitude is very important here. It will come through in your interactions and transform the nature of them. A negative attitude, as we've discussed, can be poisonous in this step. If you are not positive, why would an employer hire you? Maintain a positive attitude at all times, even if you're fearful or nervous. Recruiters tend to avoid candidates who exude a negative demeanor or complain about the difficulties of the job market. On the flip side, there are many candidates who have gone through the same hardships, but when they are interviewing, they are positive. That positivity is contagious.

Save the pain and frustration of your job search for someone else. Don't bring it into the room with you. Of course, nervousness in an interview is natural. It's okay to experience that as long as you have the right attitude. And remember, the worst thing that can happen is that they don't offer you the job. Even if they don't offer you a position, send the person who interviewed you a thank you note and wish them well. It will establish you as an individual with impeccable manners and even confidence. You will put the idea in their mind that you'd be a good person to represent their company. The next time there is an opening, you'll be far more likely to be considered.

Here Is What I Want You To Do For Me

When the interviewer is concluding the interview, this is your cue to let him know that you are interested in the job and to ask what the next step is. Don't ask about compensation and benefits. Instead, let the interviewer bring up these topics. Often times, interviewers will ask the applicant what compensation he or she is seeking. This is an area where many job seekers make a crucial misstep.

When interviewers ask this question, a lot of interviewees will say they don't know, or cite a figure based on guesswork that is too high or too low. They erroneously believe that if they admit they will accept any type of offer, they will seem more appealing to the person doing the hiring. In fact, many people believe that their hardship or mortgage or childcare responsibilities will entice prospective employers. But this desperation invariably has the opposite effect, especially in the case of expressing a willingness to be paid very little. It acts as a red flag that makes employers consider that you may be under-qualified. Of course, the other pitfall job seekers step into is asking for too much money, which will make employers hire someone less expensive. What both extremes have in common is that they illustrate a lack of preparedness and a lack of awareness about the position that you seek.

What will land you in strong consideration is saying, "This is what I would like to be paid based on my experience and what I can do for you." Follow this statement by stating a salary range: $40,000 to $60,000 for example. It is important to add, "I am negotiable." Conveying this information impresses the idea that you know your worth, but you are also flexible. You also leave the door open for your prospective employer to make you a decent offer.

In order to arrive at your figure, there is a vast abundance of information available on the internet. There are numerous websites that can tell you the salaries of people doing the job you're applying for in your geographic area. Often times, the salary range is even made available in the job posting itself. Either way, it's necessary to show up for the interview with a realistic figure in mind. Once they've decided you're the best candidate for the position, it's your chance to share that information.

To illustrate these three key steps, let's look at a quick example. (Pay attention, because there will be a pop quiz afterwards!)

Bill and James both have the same qualifications, educational background and experience. They are identical in almost every way. In fact, for the sake of argument, let's say they are twins, sharing the same job seekers' DNA.

They both apply for the same job at a huge, multinational firm and are both selected for an interview with three of the employees of the company. In the interview, Bill tells the interviewing manager about his impressive educational background, professional expertise, and experience. But he complains about his previous boss, and neglects to mention all of his own achievements for the company. Also, Bill's resume doesn't reflect his experience that would be most pertinent to the job he's interviewing for. On top of all this, when asked how much he expects to be paid, Bill throws himself on his sword and says he'd accept anything, as he's been unemployed for a long time and is experiencing financial hardship.

James, on the other hand, utilizes the interview as a platform to explain all that he will be able to do for the company if given the opportunity, based on his background. James' resume and cover letter have been targeted specifically to the job he seeks. And lastly, when James is asked about his salary requirements, he gives them a range, adding that he is negotiable and flexible.

Who do you think is more likely to be hired? If you answered James, congratulations! You're right. James illustrated his preparedness, but most importantly, he clearly established himself as the ideal candidate by laying out what he could do for his new employer. As I mentioned earlier, the employer is most interested in what you can do for them. They really don't care about your background, except with respect to how you can use it for their benefit. They already have your resume and know enough about you to decide to interview you in the first place.

Employers are selfish and are only looking out for their own interests. They don't really care about you, your feelings or your current financial situation. They don't want to hear about your obligations, your bills that you can't pay, or that your house is about to be foreclosed on. All they care about is what you can offer them with your personal services for fixed amounts of time – days, weeks, or months – to help them achieve their objectives. This information is not meant to douse your enthusiasm. In fact, I mention it to simplify things for you. It will help you distill your performance in the interview to one clear message: what you can offer them.

How Do You Know Exactly What To Offer The Employer?

Now that you know what you need to express in the interview, the question becomes, "how do you know exactly what to offer the employer?" This is a fact-finding mission that begins with your initial communication with the job hirer. You should be getting as much clarity about the position as possible from the get-go. Don't be afraid to ask a few questions about the position in your calls or emails with the company. Once you've done that and your other research, you will be able to establish what you can offer the employer.

As simple as this may sound, this is where the majority of job seekers fumble. They use the interview as an opportunity to discuss their past experiences and education rather than selling the interviewer on the job they will do for the company.

How Do You Get The Employer To Want To Interview You So You Can Tell The Employer What You Have to Offer?

So far we've assumed that getting an interview is a foregone conclusion, but as many job seekers can attest to, just getting the interview is a challenge. So, how do you get yourself in front of the hiring committee?

Many people take the approach of sending the employer a resume and hoping they get interviewed based on that. Unfortunately, this is what thousands of other people are doing. Most likely, the resume will literally get thrown in the trash. (Or, as the case may be, moved to the trash on someone's computer desktop.)

In most companies, there is an individual who works in Human Resources and is in charge of selecting the appropriate candidates for a job opening. This person is a gatekeeper. It's vital that you get through this gatekeeper in order to get to the hiring manager. How do you make this happen? I'll share with you a method that has proven to work in countries where the unemployment rate is 70 percent, as well as in certain European countries, where the unemployment is 15 to 25 percent. It will work even better in the United States, where the unemployment rate is 7 to 12 percent, depending on where you reside.

So how do we do it? How do we break through to this HR person? Well first, we need to stop considering this person an enemy. Bear in mind that most HR staff members receive hundreds of resumes a day. It is very difficult for them to review all of these resumes to choose the candidate who would make the best fit for the position. In some companies, these gatekeepers aren't even trained on how to wade through all the resumes they receive. So, with all that in mind, how do you get noticed in a crowd?

I'll answer with an example. I received my masters in business administration (MBA) in 2002, at the height of the "dot com" recession. At the time, I was based in Denver, Colorado. Denver is a beautiful city with lots of sunshine and clear skies, even in the middle of the winter. There's so much to do outside, including skiing, hiking, biking, and other types of entertainment. I also found the people to be very warm and welcoming there. Unfortunately, it was also one of the hardest hit cities during the recession, due in large part to the number of high tech and telecommunications companies based there. Companies like World Com and Global Crossing were all going bust and thousands of employees were laid off in the process.

So you can imagine how difficult it was being new to the job market, fresh out of college, with very few jobs being advertised. I remember going to a career fair and asking a woman representing one of the companies how many people had applied for the position she was there to fill. She informed me that at last count, she had received 1,503 resumes *by email alone.* She hadn't even counted all of the resumes that were handed to her that very day at the career fair. She then asked me if I had a resume for her that she could place in her file. I told her I didn't have a resume for her folder, but I did have the knowledge, desire, and ability to do the job that was being offered by a company... "and here is how." After outlining what my approach would be for the new job, five minutes later, she asked me what my availability was to come to work the following Monday.

I of course said I was available, and handed her my resume. (You didn't think I would actually attend a job fair without a resume!) What I said to her in those five minutes that changed everything wasn't magical, gimmicky or sales-y. It was exactly what was in my resume. But rather than hand her a resume she would never look at, I used that time to go over it with her while I had her full attention. I related to her what I had to offer based on the job description.

In the course of my job search, I have found other, more "old fashioned" ways of contacting companies that have proven very effective. I have sent many companies I was interested in working for a targeted email and cover letter, outlining what I would do for the company. But I also sent the same resume and pitch for my services via courier and fax. What I've discovered is that a lot of people have given up on using faxes as a means of applying for work, and almost no one uses a courier service like FedEx or UPS to send in their resume. But using this approach assures that it will be a physical object in someone's hands. This tactile experience makes it much more difficult to simply ignore or throw away. By using this technique to apply for several jobs, I was able to get interviews and receive a few managerial job offers without having any MBA experience. All you have to do is think differently (much like the Apple slogan, "Think different").

Now that I've illustrated the three most common mistakes of job seekers and the top three things that successful job seekers do, we're ready for the next step!

Getting Started With The Job Seeker System

Now, I'm going to share with you a profoundly useful Job Getting System. The system is an excellent tool, but it will only work if you use it and commit to it! It can't work with minimal effort on your part. If you show up for this with willingness and enthusiasm, you will soon master the strategies I outline here and get the job you desire.

What I will do is show you how to think differently. Using the new ideas and strategies I will discuss, you will join the ranks of my thousands of other clients over the past fifteen years who quickly received job offers. Your educational level or lack thereof, professional background, or the local unemployment rate will not be obstacles. In the pages ahead, I will outline exactly how you will be able to master each of these steps to move forward professionally and get the job you truly deserve.

1. Get the Courage to Get the Job You Desire.

2. How to Create an Effective Resume

3. Creative Ways to Get Selected, Your Resume Selected and to Get Interviewed

4. How to Effectively Tell Your Prospective Employer What You Have to Offer

5. How to Effectively Interview Over the Phone or In Person

6. How Not to Be Nervous or Afraid During an Interview

7. The Three Most Effective Ways to Apply For a Job

8. How to Use Social Media to Apply For and Get the Job You Want

9. How to Use the Law of Averages in Getting a Job

10. How to Be In the Right State of Mind to Apply For and Get the Job You Desire

11. And Much More...

Your state of mind is perhaps the most important item on this list. If you're not in the proper state of mind, you're actually fighting two battles: one with the job market and one with yourself.

So far, I've only discussed how my Job Getting System has worked for me. At this point, I think it would be useful to share with you a story of how this system impacted the life of one of my clients, Susan. I first encountered Susan literally begging for money on the streets. I saw Susan standing on the street with her cardboard sign saying she was hungry and homeless, and wondered if my system could work for someone in such a dire situation. Susan had lost all hope at this point. If you consider her reality for a moment, it truly is the epitome of hopelessness. No one who still has any hope could resort to something this extreme as begging on the street corner. Every day on my way home from work, I would see Susan and give her whatever change I had. One day, I finally asked her if she was interested in my help with getting her a job that would enable her to get back on her feet. She said yes, and we began meeting several times a week at a local coffee shop. I began gradually sharing with her the information that I had gleaned from experts and CEOs over the years. Susan wasn't the most intelligent person I've worked with, but that didn't matter. She displayed her commitment by showing up on time for each of our sessions. After a few weeks, she said she was ready to start looking for a job, using the information and tools I had imparted her. I also gave her access to my paid membership website, which she was able to log onto for free at the library. She promised she would call me if she had any questions.

Then, something happened: Susan disappeared from the street corner. She was nowhere to be found for several weeks. Since she didn't have a phone, there was no way for me to contact her. After several months of not seeing Susan, I finally saw her one night when I was on my way home from a speaking engagement. Unfortunately, she was back at the very same street corner. I was shocked, confused, and full of questions. I asked her why I hadn't heard from her. She replied that she'd lost my number, but she actually did get a job using my Job Getting System. She confessed, however, that she actually liked begging on the street corner better. She said that she liked meeting and interacting with hundreds of people a day, and that she enjoyed the free time she had from "working" on the street. So she decided to quit her job after a couple of months and return to the street.

As you can imagine, I was speechless. But regardless of Susan's choices, this turn of events reaffirmed that my system can work for literally anyone, even someone who would prefer begging to working!

This story is a demonstration of one of my job getting techniques, affirming What I Will Do For You. But rather than simply taking my word for it, I thought it would be helpful to read some of my prior clients' experiences.

Norman Nelson

Lakewood, CA

My name is Norman Nelson. I'd been out of work for a number of years when I met George through a mutual friend. What I found from my work with George is the importance of having a positive focus on your professional direction. If you have doubts and negativity in your life, you'll find it very difficult to get a job. You need to have courage, confidence and a belief in yourself.

At the time I met George, I had three children at home and my wife wasn't working. I'd been laid off in the past, but with the economy what it was, I knew this time was going to be much, much more difficult.

It only took me a few weeks to read the materials, and within a *month, I was shocked to get more responses to the resumes I'd been sending out. People started calling me and were interested in talking to me more about my abilities and my background. Shortly thereafter, I received a call for an interview and was hired within a couple of days of that interview. I totally credit George's information with this turn of events. He off*ers simple step-by-step instruction that you can easily follow. Along the way, you'll become instilled with the mentality that you can do this and that you can get a job that's right for you.

Brian Grant

Chicago, IL

After being out of a job for six months, I was really getting discouraged. I'm so glad I discovered George's Job Getting System. This system landed me the job of my dreams. After purchasing and going through the web series video course, I was able to develop the confidence to go after and get my current job, which is in a highly competitive field. Not only did it transform my resume and application process, I was able to interview confidently. I even used George's tools to help negotiate my current salary, which is so much higher than what I would have accepted without George's direction. I've become adept at communicating effectively over the phone and in person and using social media to my advantage. I just want to thank George for his great work. I'm sure that anyone else who uses his system will have great results as well!

Karolina Applegate

Germantown, Maryland

Before I discovered George's Job Getting System, I had been out of work for a while and tried a lot of video courses that, simply put, were a waste of time. Those experiences made me a bit skeptical at first. But through working George's system, I was able to cultivate the confidence necessary to pursue my new dream job. I learned how to create an impeccable resume and cover letter. I was so grateful to find myself interviewing for jobs without the fear of rejection.

Dave Thomas

Toronto, Canada

I'm so grateful to have discovered George's course! Regardless of the unemployment rate where you are, these methods will help establish yourself as a desirable candidate. I was astonished with how quickly things turned around for me. After months of unemployment, I was in the position of choosing between two job offers. I couldn't believe it!

*****

At this point, some of you have read this far and may still be thinking, "this isn't for me." But if you want to get a job in this economy, this system is absolutely for you. The information presented here is the result of fifteen years of research, conversations with experts and professionals, and my own experiences working with clients. You could spend hundreds of hours doing your own footwork but still not discover the secrets that will help you go from job seeker to employee. I hasten to add that no job hunting system has a 100% success rate, but that's because my Job Getting System works only for those who use it.

Many of my clients ask me, "how long will it take for me to get a job?" While this timeline varies from person to person, my top clients received job offers in 30 days or less. My system is special because it isn't about doing the same things the same way that all the other so-called experts tell you to. This will work for people in any industry, no matter how niche. It is based on fundamentals of business and human behavior.

In every culture and industry in the world, employers behave the same. They will hire anyone that will enable them to achieve their objective as an organization.

3 Key Things To Do While Reading This Book

As I said before, this Job Getting System is a toolbox. It will work for anyone. However, having an open mind will increase the speed and strength of your transformation. I'm not even asking you to go into this with 100% certainty that it will work for you. Doubt is normal and a part of the human experience. What I do ask is that you ignore the voice in your head that is saying, "This won't work." During periods of stress, especially in periods of protracted unemployment, that negative thinking can be exacerbated. And yet it doesn't serve you or your goals at all. Learning to ignore that critical, doubting voice will enable you to proceed through the Job Getting System with much more ease and flow.

Secondly, don't worry. I know how difficult this situation is. I've talked to thousands of unemployed people over the past fifteen years of coaching, and I know very well what life is like for someone without a job. But you will get through this and come out the other side. You will be able to go on vacation again, make the home improvements you've been putting off, and take your family out for dinner someplace you love. This book is the bridge that will take you to that place. But instead of interpreting the suggestion to not worry as "I mustn't worry," look at it like this: you *deserve* to not worry. You are in a challenging position, one that has been created by external factors for most of you. Berating yourself, catastrophizing, and flooding your body with stress doesn't do anyone any good. Many of us confuse worry with footwork. It simply isn't. It certainly won't make that new job come any closer to you. So whatever you can do to reduce your worry, do it. If you feel like you absolutely need to worry about this, give yourself ten minutes a day to do that. Whenever the worries creep into your consciousness, say to yourself, "I already did my ten minutes today. I'll listen to you the next time." And continue with something productive or relaxing.

Never ever forget that you too can succeed! You've been doing so much on your own, but now that you have the Job Getting System, you will be able to relax in the knowledge that I have a proven track record of helping thousands of people get jobs. This is also a good time to remind yourself that you've succeeded in many areas before. You've been hired before and made contributions to your workplace, your family, and your community. During the course of their unemployment, a lot of my clients have built up an erroneous narrative in their minds that they're lazy or chronically unable to rise to life's challenges. This is just not true. You will succeed and thrive again. In fact, all of the discouragement you've experienced will be transformed to gold once you've moved through this difficult time and see yourself as a person who can persevere through the hardest of situations.

To summarize, remind yourself every day to do the following:

- **Have an Open Mind**

- **Don't Worry**

- **Remember That You Too Can Succeed!**

3 Key Things Not To Do While Reading This Book

I would be surprised if this were your first time reading a book, article, or blog about how to get a job. Nothing brings out single-minded focus in someone like unemployment. Surely some of the ideas here may seem familiar, but most are totally unique. This isn't just my opinion, that's based on the feedback I've received from thousands of (now employed) clients. An analogy I like to use is to compare this book to someone asking you if you're hungry when you're utterly famished. From the time you were a child, people have asked you if you're hungry countless times. But if you haven't eaten in a few days, asking you "Are you hungry?" takes on an entirely different resonance. Sometimes the context just has to be different to benefit from a similar message you've heard before.

Don't succumb to external pressures. Friends and family – who are well meaning in their own way – may make sarcastic comments about you going about your job search this way. These comments may have the disastrous affect of dimming your enthusiasm. While some of their jabs may ring true, bear in mind that sarcasm has never gotten anyone a job (except perhaps for a comedian). While you're reading this book and digesting the concepts I lay out, give yourself time to work the tools presented here before you talk about this with someone who may try to undermine your confidence. Let other people's biases and doubts remain theirs. You don't need to take them on.

My third commandment is "Thou Shalt Not Skim." If you simply read this book passively as you would a paperback you bought to the beach, this won't work for you. This book is a blueprint for your new behaviors that will lead you to the job of your dreams. This requires shifts in your thinking and attitudes as well as your actions. Passing glances at the Job

Getting System simply will not serve you. To get the most out of this book, commit to it fully.

In the following 30 days, commit to avoiding:

- **Thinking That You've Heard It All Before**

- **Succumbing To External Pressure**

- **Skimming Through the Book**

"Register now for a FREE online WEBINAR on

How To Get A Job In 30 Days Or Less!

and receive a FREE Special Report on

7 Great Jobs That Are Always Hiring

Click the link below..."

www.helpingfeet.com/webinar

Things You Must Do Before You Start Looking For A Job

The first thing you must do before your search is to get in the right state of mind. If you believe you can get a job, that belief will change the nature of your interactions. You will be infused with a level of confidence that will make you much more desirable to prospective employers. Of course the converse is also true: desperation and negativity can often repel situations or people that could help us. As Henry Ford said, "If you think you can do a thing or think you can't do a thing, you're right."

So I encourage you to start your job search with a sales job. I want you to become an expert at selling yourself on the idea that you are marketable. You are sellable. You have so much to offer. It's only a matter of time before an employer will be able to recognize that. By the end of this section, you will have a clear idea on precisely how to accomplish this.

The battle with ourselves starts with the limiting beliefs we have about ourselves. All of us carry limiting beliefs. They act as filters for how we perceive our reality. They exist because the human mind likes to form them to simplify our lives. The brain is hard-wired to be pain avoidant, and these limiting beliefs have actually been created to spare us pain or embarrassment. They allow us to make sense of complex and especially disappointing situations.

For example, a limiting belief that almost every person I've talked to has is "finding a job is ____." You can fill in the blank with any number of negative adjectives: difficult, draining, impossible, exhausting, and on and on. The other especially toxic mantra (or anti-mantra) I hear so often is "There are no jobs out there."

Of course, your restless mind isn't content to just make

statements about the external world. It knows where you're most vulnerable and makes the limiting beliefs specifically about you. "I can't get a job because _____." I've heard just about every reason in that blank. It's where job hunters' creativity, pessimism and sense of total uniqueness seem to collide. The most common responses are that I'm too young, too old, not qualified, not educated, or my race or religion would make people hire someone else.

Another commonly held limiting belief is "I can't succeed in getting a job until I have _____." Generally this branches off into people feeling they don't have enough time, experience, or education.

The most crippling belief is "That's just the way things are." This has its many variations but it always boils down to "I can't get a job and that's just the way things are." I say that this belief is the most formidable foe because it presents the strongest barrier to get into the right state of mind. It reveals a point of view that the world is fixed in a very rigid way and that there is no possibility beyond the setbacks and disappointments you've grown accustomed to.

So where do our limiting beliefs come from? They build up in our consciousness from interactions and events in our past. We identify with them, we agree with them, and we are afraid to argue with them because it feels like we are arguing with ourselves. They've been ingrained into us and we turn to them reflexively whenever we go through something that challenges us, like being jobless.

How To Overcome Limiting Beliefs

But how can we overcome these limiting beliefs? First, you have to identify your own limiting beliefs. What are you insecure about? What is the worst-case scenario that could possibly happen to you? Write them down and say them out loud. I recommend saying it out loud, because this is how your healthier, conscious mind will recognize the fallacy of your limiting beliefs. It may be scary at first, but these ideas are weeds in your garden and they need to be uprooted. In the course of saying these limiting beliefs out loud, a lot of my clients see that there is no proof or factual basis for them.

Ask yourself: what purpose do my limiting beliefs serve? Does this belief that is limiting serve any positive purpose in your life? Does it help you move forward? Does it help you get the job you desire? Obviously, the answer is a huge NO. But for most of us, limiting beliefs are like a security blanket. They've been with us so long that we can't see that they've lost their usefulness. But every day you're job hunting, you can start to reverse this pattern of thinking by taking this next action.

Flip your limiting beliefs around. Give yourself permission to do whatever you need to do to reverse your negative beliefs, including playing opposite with them. For instance, if your negative belief is "I can't find a job," say to yourself, "The perfect employer is looking for me right now." This isn't a mind trick, but a way of reminding yourself of what is really true. For each of your negative beliefs, there is a healthy, empowering converse belief that will serve you well.

No Fear

In the thousands of clients I've worked with, all of them are dealing with some level of fear. A crucial part of my Job Getting System is eliminating the fear you've been battling with to redirect your energy to getting the job you truly desire.

So what is fear? Fear is emotional distress that stems from worry and indecision. Fear causes intellectual paralysis and impedes your problem-solving intellect. It bars you from applying your skills and experiences to just about any situation.

Most fears come from considering new perspectives. It is especially acute when we have incomplete information that makes us worry and become indecisive. Some of my clients have had their fears stop them from a whole host of important activities. Some were too afraid to send out networking emails or ask for help creating a resume. Others felt they weren't good in interviews so they had come to fear the whole interview process.

How To Eliminate Your Fear

Most fears stem from a feeling of being unprepared to handle a new or unfamiliar situation. People tend to futurize and envision a worst-case scenario by filling in "facts" that aren't actually real. We can reduce our fears by reminding ourselves that it's okay to consider a different perspective.

Another way to eliminate your fears is by having a clearly defined plan and following it. Being unemployed makes planning our lives extremely difficult. But the tools and instructions of my Job Getting System are your plan that will help manage your time and efforts in a way that will serve you as best as possible. It will eliminate the guesswork and the burden of having to make difficult choices.

Perhaps the most vital instruction in improving your mindset is to STOP over-analyzing! Stop second-guessing yourself. Stop scrutinizing that ambiguous email from a recruiter. Stop trying to deduce what the other people in the waiting area are thinking about you before your interview. Keep it simple and stay in the area of what is factual. All the wondering and self-induced anxiety is a waste of your time. It's really just a way of your mind trying to occupy itself, so do whatever you can to fill your mind with positive, constructive thoughts.

How To Eliminate Fear And Negativity

I've outlined ways to improve your mental state in a somewhat general way, but let's get as clear as possible about how to help maintain a positive attitude through the daily challenges you face as a job seeker.

View your thoughts and your mind as a body that requires healthy nutrients. In this analogy, the nutrients aren't food but supportive ideas and experiences.

INPUT SOURCE	MESSAGE
NEWS	THERE ARE NO JOBS IT'S NOT SAFE DANGER
TABLOIDS, GOSSIP, REALITY TV	PEOPLE ARE BAD PEOPLE CAN'T BE TRUSTED
TALK RADIO	THERE ARE NO JOBS LET'S BLAME SOMEONE

This chart reflects the way many people's negative ideas are formed. The news – whether it be from the radio, TV, or the internet – is dominated by bad news, because bad news sells. If you sit in front of the TV for half an hour and are bombarded with stories about foreclosures, unemployment statistics, and rising poverty, how strong is your enthusiasm for your job hunt? How cheerful will you be when you go write that cover letter or attend that networking event afterwards? Of course, on top of the economic stories, we're reminded of what a dangerous and unsafe world it is by stories of war and crime.

The other major sources of information in this era are tabloid journalism, gossip, and reality television. While this encompasses a wide range of internet, print, and electronic media, a recurring message one derives from absorbing this intellectual junk food is that people are bad. Just as damaging, if not more so, is the message that people can't be trusted. Reality TV is a huge booster of this last idea. The most common "storyline" on those types of programs is that everyone is always talking behind someone else's back.

Another way we feed our minds is via talk radio. It's an easy companion when we're driving or just want some background noise when we're at home. The crux of most talk radio nowadays is being argumentative and critical. On topical shows where they discuss a subject and have guests on with opposing viewpoints, the message that there are no jobs still persists, but the focus becomes fighting over who is to blame.

Your input source determines your state of mind. If you feel depressed and discouraged, some of that could be fueled by the input sources you're consuming. The sum total message of the types of radio, TV and internet listed above is "Be afraid. Be worried. The world is uncertain. There is so much hate in the world."

If you want to change the way you think - which, as established, you must do in order to get a job – you must change your input source immediately. So let's flip it around and get the message we want!

Suggested Steps To Eliminate Fear And Negativity

To discuss how to fuel your mind with the reverse message, I'll reverse the order of the last chart. We will start with the message we want and follow it with the ideal input source.

MESSAGE	INPUT SOURCE
YOU CAN GET A JOB!	MOTIVATIONAL BOOKS, VIDEOS, OR ONLINE PROGRAMS HELPINGFEET.COM MEMBERSHIP SITE
PEOPLE CAN BE TRUSTED PEOPLE ARE GOOD	CHURCH SUCCESS MAGAZINES PEER GROUPS HELPFUL WEBSITES
IF OTHERS CAN HAVE SUCCESS, SO CAN I	SUCCESS STORIES ON WEBSITES, IN MAGAZINES

Obviously, the most important message that you want to have circulating in your mind all the time is that you can get a job. To this end, it's helpful to read motivational books, or to watch inspirational videos or online programs. If you aren't already a member, I highly encourage you to join my HelpingFeet.com website, which is full of important information and invaluable tips for job seekers.

Another negative message we discussed earlier is that people are bad. The opposite of that is that people are good, or can be trusted. This is an important message because unemployment so often leads to a sense of isolation. That can be worsened by seeing everyone as a competitor. If you have a spiritual or religious inclination, this is a good time to lean on that foundation. If church is a place you feel inspired, go often. Reading business success stories can also be helpful. Relying on trusted friends is also important. Your friends care about you and don't see you as your unemployment struggles, but as someone who is bravely walking through a difficult situation. Soak up that image and you will feel better about yourself. Also, feel free to visit any uplifting or fun websites. Avoid the types of websites I referred to earlier which traffic in bad news or celebrity journalism.

Another important thing to remind yourself is, "If others can have success finding a job, so can I." So often, others' success makes us feel inadequate. Or we have absorbed the idea that jobs are so scarce that someone else's gain is our loss. Instead, the biggest gift you can give yourself is being authentically happy for people who get a job. It's a sign that it's doable, and more specifically, that you in particular can do it.

By following these action items, you can become infused with hope, desire, and enthusiasm. You will cease to compare yourself to others and realize that this unemployment is just a period in time that has been difficult but is not permanent. By feeling better, you will feel courage, confidence, and a new feeling of fearlessness. By switching the messages and the input source, you will come to a new place where you are in the right state of mind. That new state of mind will absolutely show. People will want to be around you because that level of confidence is far more conducive to a balanced and energetic workplace.

If you know from experience that you have positive input sources that aren't in the chart above, by all means, use those too!

Determine The Exact Job You Desire

After someone has been without work for a long time, they usually become resigned to taking any job, even something they really don't like. But by using my Job Getting System, you won't just get another dead end job. You can find something that you're really excited about!

I want to share with you an experience I had when I was looking for a job. I have a mechanical engineering degree and an MBA. While I was studying for my engineering degree, I had to get an internship. There was a manufacturing internship that I wasn't really interested in, but I applied for it anyway just to get a job. I performed poorly in the interview because I just didn't want to work there. Surprisingly, they hired me, most likely because they were desperate to hire someone and I just happened to be there at the right time.

I'm not really a morning person, but for this job I had to be there at 5:30 AM. Another strike against this position was that I'm not really interested in the manufacturing side of engineering. I'm much more inspired by the design and management side of engineering. The only reason I made it to work on time was because my friend Paul, who loved the manufacturing side of engineering, had to be there at 5:30 every morning too. He literally dragged me to work every day. (Actually, I was the one with the car, but I couldn't let him down so I picked him up on time every day.)

So there I was, drowsy and disinterested on the manufacturing floor. It's a miracle I never injured myself, as I almost lost my hands several times. Wisely, my higher-ups banned me from the machines and transferred me to the labs, at the other end of the facility. The experience was one of the worst jobs of my life and it turned out the feeling was mutual. At the end of my three months, my supervisor told me I was the worst employee he'd ever seen in his twenty years. Full of bravado, I replied that I wasn't an employee, just a poorly paid intern. Frankly, I think the only reason I wasn't fired was because my buddy Paul helped me get there on time and covered up for me countless times.

After that experience, I promised myself I would never apply for a job like that again. Now, do you think I kept my promise? If you guessed "no," give yourself a gold star. But fortunately for me, every time I went to an interview where I wasn't passionate about the job, I did badly and wound up not getting hired. I guess it showed on my face or came across in my attitude.

Again, if you have been laid off, this is a time to get a job that you truly desire. In fact, it's actually easier to excel at looking for and applying for a job that you truly desire.

What Is The Exact Job You Desire?

I had a client named Thomas, who was an accountant. But his true passion was customer service. He'd only studied accounting at the suggestion of his father, who said that accountants always seemed to have an easier time getting jobs. Thomas had recently been laid off from an accounting job, but instead of looking for another accounting job, he decided to look for one in customer service at an accounting firm. He could still use his accounting skills, but put the focus on customer service. He loved talking to people on the phone, helping them resolve issues. It was his passion, and he was able to find it in the industry he was already in.

In Thomas's case, this professional transition was relatively easy. But even if you need to change industries completely, you can still find the job you desire and I will show you how in the following chapters. But, first start by writing down the exact type of job you desire and not one based on your experience or qualifications. There's power in putting it down on paper.

Do You Have The Required Skill Set Or Experience?

This is an obstacle that's necessary to consider, but not one that has the power to bar you from pursuing something that you want to do. Formulate a plan on how you will achieve the qualifications you need. Sometimes it's a relatively simple solution, like taking an online course or attending a seminar. **But the key thing to remember is that what we are passionate about is always something we already know how and love to do**. Your learning curve will be very fast, regardless of the industry you're in now.

Jose was another client of mine. He was a construction worker, but he was actually not very good at the actual construction work. His real passion was managing construction projects. Once Jose got clear on what he wanted to do, all he had to do was spend a couple weeks learning a project management program geared toward the construction industry. With that in hand, Jose was able to get hired at a large commercial construction company doing exactly what he loved to do.

So many of my clients believed that it would be impossible to find satisfaction in their current industry, but often times wound up finding something they were passionate about by working in a different capacity in their same field. Sometimes it's just a matter of thinking a little differently to get the job that's right for you.

Are You Willing To Relocate Or Commute?

If you're open to the idea of residing in a new state, region, or country, the chances of getting the job you desire increases significantly. There are places in the United States where the job market is surprisingly robust.

For example, Williston, North Dakota, is one such place. There is at this present time actually a hiring frenzy due to the oil fields and drilling activities. There are a ton of available jobs there in every possible services area. Employers are looking for people in every position you can imagine, and I'm not even talking about all the available technical jobs. There is approximately a three percent unemployment rate, which essentially translates to full employment. Their only problem now is finding accommodations for their new residents.

Another client of mine lives in Las Vegas, but found his dream job in Los Angeles, California. His solution? He commutes 4 to 6 hours per week to Los Angeles and stays there Monday through Friday. For now, it works and he's happy doing it.

Determine The Exact Amount You Want To Earn

Having a figure in mind when you apply for a job is crucial to getting hired. If you ask for a salary that's too low, the hiring manager may think you don't value yourself or are under qualified for the position. So it's important to have an accurate assessment of what salary you should ask for based on your skills, experience and education.

Also, you need to know how much you realistically need to live on and not go below that amount. Many of my clients are incredibly vague about what their expenses really are, and tend to underestimate how much they actually require to live. This can result in what I call "the winners' curse." This is when a job seeker goes through the protracted effort of applying, interviewing, and accepting a job, to only then realize that they've agreed to a salary that won't meet their needs.

Remember, you get what you ask for in life. Whatever you think you deserve you will most likely earn. ***You earn your pay first in your mind before you earn it in person.*** So don't be underpaid and undervalued. You deserve more.

One of my clients, Shirley, got a retail job offer with a salary that was less than what she could ideally live on. Her pay would only cover her rent. All the rest, including food, gas, utilities, and entertainment she'd have to figure out on her own. So unfortunately, Shirley had to start all over and begin the application process at other jobs. If she'd known what she needed to make to begin with, she would never have gone down the road of applying for a job that was such a poor fit for her.

HOW TO DETERMINE THE EXACT SALARY YOU WANT

There is an abundance of information available about what salaries one can expect in a certain job. Payscale.com is an excellent resource that I refer my clients to. The website has a questionnaire that asks you a series of detailed questions and calculates a salary for you based on the information you provide.

Of course, having honest, well-informed friends in the same field who can provide salary information is also extremely valuable. They key with these calculations is to also know what the take-home pay will be after payroll deductions. There are numerous websites out there that can help determine this figure accurately. An internet search with the words "net pay calculator" will yield many useful results.

Past experience can also inform your salary quote if you're looking in the same industry you've worked in. There are also numerous governmental and union positions where the salary information is publicly available.

I know it's tempting to throw your hands up in the air and say, "I'll take anything," but having certainty around money creates a different energy that will show prospective employers that you deserve the salary you're asking for.

SETTING GOALS AND DEVELOPING YOUR PLAN

In the course of pursuing a new job, many people make the mistake of identifying their need for a job and jumping right into the application process. They all but overlook the crucial bridge between these two actions, which is setting your goals and developing a plan of action. It's necessary to set your goals, even before you start reaching out to prospective employers.

As I mentioned before, there is an art and a science to getting a job. Setting a goal falls under the "science" category of job seeking. By doing this, you create the possibility of getting the job you truly desire. This goal setting has a power to it that makes you psychologically ready to receive the right job, one that lines up with your belief that you deserve to feel excited to go to work in the morning.

Your goal is specific to you. For the purpose of this discussion, I'll use the following goal as an example:

"My goal is to get a job in 30 days that will allow me to pay my bills and provide for my family. This will be achieved by using the information in the book How To Get A Job In 30 Days! *and on the HelpingFeet.com membership website."*

This is a pretty straightforward goal that most of my clients express in one form or another. But it also contains four elements that your goal must have. They are as follows:

- What

- When

- Why

- How

For something to be a goal as opposed to a wish or a daydream, it has to contain those four components: what, when, why and how. The "what" in this case is "to get a job in 30 days." The "when" is "30 days." Why? To pay your bills and provide for your family. The "how" is by using the tools in this book and on the Helping Feet website.

I worked with a client once who was a single man in his 20s who came from a wealthy family. He had difficulty identifying a goal for himself. With no one else to worry about supporting, and access to family money to help him with his overhead, he couldn't relate to the goal above that I showed him as an example. His motivation for getting a job was actually to buy a luxury Mercedes that his parents refused to finance.

So we simply altered the goal to reflect his true desire, and it became "To get a job in 30 days so I can purchase the Mercedes I want using the tools in the book *How to Get a Job in 30 Days* and on the Helping Feet website." The particulars of your goal don't matter as long as the four questions – what, when, why and how – are all addressed. If you want to give yourself shorter or longer than 30 days, that's fine too, as long as that timeline is clear for you. The whole point of the goal setting is really to change your psychology and get the ball rolling on your job search.

Write your goal down. Once you've written it, it's very important that you read it every morning and every night. Place it somewhere so it's plainly visible throughout the day: taped to your mirror, on your refrigerator, or next to your computer are some places that have worked for my clients. This will help your goal permeate into your subconscious, where it will become a force that will guide your actions toward achieving it, even when your conscious mind is focused on something else.

SETTING YOUR GOALS AND PLANNING

Setting your goals is a foundational piece of my Job Getting System. Now we're going to discuss how we actually achieve those goals. In order to do so, we must create what I call a master plan.

A master plan covers everything that we must do in order to achieve the goal that we desire. Here are the components of your master plan:

MASTER PLAN

- **Getting Ready**

- **Search and Apply**

- **Interview**

- **Follow Up**

- **Rinse and Repeat**

The first step, getting ready, can involve a variety of important activities. For you it may include buying a new suit for interviews or creating different resumes for different skill sets you possess.

The next step comes after you've gathered together your references and recommendation letters and have revised your resume to include your most marketable skills and experience. It's the actual search and application process. Your search and application process becomes a direct, specific reflection of your goal.

Once you've contacted a prospective employer with your targeted resume and cover letter, the right one will be impressed by you and ask you to come in for an interview. As we've discussed before, you need to thoroughly research the company and come prepared with a salary range to discuss in case you are asked. I also recommend giving yourself an extra half hour to get to the interview site. If you show up late for a job interview, you may as well not show up at all.

After the interview is the follow-up. This should always include a thank you note, which you should mail the day of the interview. It can also include some of your prospective employer's housekeeping items, such as a background check or drug test.

After you've gone through these steps, it's time to rinse and repeat. You need to go through this process as many times as necessary in order to achieve the goal you've written down. Of course, by now you'll have an easier time following through on this process. Your goal is in writing, in plain sight, and you're repeating it to yourself often.

This process can be represented graphically.

The figure on the left is you, the job seeker, and each step along the way represents the necessary order of you carrying out your plan. Too often clients of mine jump right into interviewing or applying without getting ready. Unfortunately, this cycle is repeated ad infinitum with the same unsuccessful results until they follow this process in its correct order. By taking actions in the correct sequence, you will come much closer to realizing your goal of getting hired within 30 days.

The other way of looking at this is by breaking down each

step and viewing it as a percentage of how far along you are on your way to achieving your goal of getting a job.

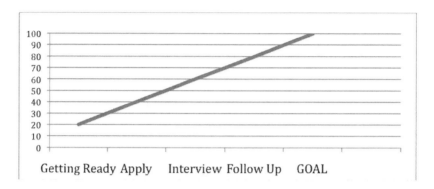

The graph begins at 0, where you haven't done anything yet except for wanting a job. At 20%, you are taking action to get ready for your job search. At 40%, you are applying for positions. At 60%, you're meeting prospective employers and being interviewed. At 80%, you're contacting the person who interviewed you for follow up. 100%, of course, is your goal. I like the numeric system of charting progress because it helps us feel less overwhelmed when we are in the process of seeking a job. It quells the inner voice that wants to say everything is hopeless by letting you see how much you've actually put forward toward your goal. Instead of having sweaty palms before an interview, you can remind yourself that you're almost 60% of the way to your new dream job!

The ascending line in the graph is what I call the **desire curve**, so named because it represents the result of your desire for a new job. If you follow the steps I've laid our for you, it will always be ascending, moving you closer to your goal based on the footwork you've been doing.

Developing Your Sub-Plan

By now you have an understanding of what the framework of your successful job search should consist of: Getting Ready, Applying, Interviewing, Following Up, Rinsing and Repeating, and ultimately, you achieve your Goal. For each of those steps, you will have a sub-plan. A sub-plan is a term that essentially means your task list.

For the first step, Getting Ready, here is a sub-plan that describes the nuts and bolts of the preparation process:

- Resume

- Cover Letter

- Recommendations, Award Letters and References

- Social Networking Profile

- Other Stuff

Having a specific, targeted resume and cover letter will be a necessity for you to achieve your goal. I also urge you to overcome any shyness and contact previous employers or colleagues for references and recommendations. Job seekers are often pleasantly surprised by the recommendation letters people write for them while they're looking for a job. It's also an opportune time to read those letters for your own morale to see how much you've contributed in prior professional settings.

You should also update your profile on LinkedIn, Facebook, Twitter, or any other social media site you use to reflect the honed, professional and marketable individual you are. Those pictures of you on that wild weekend in Las Vegas? Now would be a good time to remove them or make sure your privacy settings will keep any prospective employers from viewing them.

After you've created this sub-plan, have a specific timeline for how long each item should take to complete. As an example, your task list can look like this:

- Resume – 2 days

- Cover Letter – 1 day

- Recommendations, Award Letters and References – 3 days

- Social Networking Profile – 2 days

Getting specific with your timeline will help keep you on a schedule you can stick to. If you have a trusted friend or partner, it's a good idea to discuss your plan. This simple but effective step holds you accountable to the timeline you've set up as opposed to keeping it a secret, which makes it easier to ignore. Studies have showed that people are more likely to see through a plan if they are to be held accountable. Otherwise, it is easy to make excuses and justify to ourselves reasons why we cannot or did not do it.

"Other Stuff" sounds like a pretty nebulous category, but it's an important one. It includes having a dry-cleaned suit or other professional attire ready for last minute interviews. It's also a good idea to keep getting regular haircuts for the same reason. You're in a position where you could be called at any moment to come in for an interview right away. These small preparations can make such a huge difference in those types of situations. A lot of my clients in family situations should have a private phone number dedicated to calls from prospective employers. When they call your landline with the interview for your dream job, would you entrust your kids to take the message for you? There are cell phone plans available for as little as $20 or $30 per month, which is well worth the peace of mind that comes from not having to risk missing a golden opportunity.

By making each day about completing one of these tasks, you will feel more accomplished and enthusiastic. Prospective employers will notice that and want that energy in their work environment.

Identifying What You Need To Execute Your Plan

In this section, we're ready to get into all the things you'll need to execute your plan. I will go through each of these items, step by step, as they are crucial to your success. At the end of this section, you will know exactly how to:

- **Create an effective resume.**

- **Create a spectacular, engaging cover letter.**

- **Record an introduction video.**

- **Use recommendation and award letters effectively.**

- **As well as other small but important things to do.**

The sum total of these actions will make you ready to take on the job application process. You will impress any prospective employer with your first impression and will move to the front of the line of the candidates they're considering. So let's dive right in!

Resume

In this section we'll discuss your resume, or CV, as it's known outside of the United States. I'm not going to get into the particulars of how to write and format a resume, as there are numerous websites that can aid you with that. If you're reading this in the U.S there are governmental agencies for unemployed people that will offer free classes on this. With your resume, the key thing to note is that your resume should highlight your previous job experiences, job titles, professional qualifications, skill sets and the companies you've worked for. It's important to connect your job history as clearly as possible to the job that you're currently applying for. **Your resume is a way of saying, "Hey, look! I've successfully done before what you're saying you want in your job ad! Because I've done it successfully for someone else, I can do it again successfully *for you*."** This is key. Your resume should tell a potential employer what you can do for them. It's not about your education or qualifications, but how you use that to perform for them.

This may sound simplistic, but it's not. It will determine the way you write your resume: whether you use active, strong sentences or passive weak sentences. Let me give you an example of an active, strong sentence:

As a member of a team, I led the development of the customer service system that reduced customer complaints due to long hold times from an average of ten minutes to 3.5 minutes.

Now I'll give you an example of a passive, weak sentence:

I worked with the team on the customer service system.

As you can see, both of these statements describe the same person at the same job. But the active, strong sentence conveys a far more desirable level of involvement and performance.

Your resume must also be free of any typos. In the era of spell check, there really is no excuse for them. In some cases, spell check won't recognize some proper nouns, so after you've spell checked it, it's always a good idea to have a friend you trust give it the once-over. Any typos on your resume make you look sloppy and careless and will likely cause you to be passed over for an interview. I've spoken to several HR professionals who admitted that any typo in the resume would be grounds for them to throw it in the trash.

There are different approaches to resumes, but most fall into one of two types. The first type is a **chronological resume**. This is the most common type. In a chronological resume, you simply list your job experiences in a chronological historical pattern, starting with your most recent job history and going back to your oldest. This is great for almost everyone to use. It showcases your work history, your experiences, qualifications, and education as well as all the other information typically included in a resume. The other type of resume is a functional resume, which we will discuss later in this section.

On the following page I've provided an example of a chronological resume template that I will break down for you.

Your Name

Street Address · City, State or Province

Phone Number · e-mail address

Objective or Summary_____

A resume Objective or Summary can help describe the value you bring to a prospective employer and entice a hiring manager to read your resume.

Professional Experience_____

Financial Manager   **5 years**

Helping Feet Company – Los Angeles

- Action Words + Keywords + Skills + Knowledge

- Be specific using numbers and percentages

Job Title   **years**

Company and Location

- Action Words + Keywords + Skills + Knowledge

- Be specific using numbers and percentages

Job Title   **years**

Company and Location

- Action Words + Keywords + Skills + Knowledge

- Be specific using numbers and percentages

Relevant Skills_____

Skill Group or Title: List skills here.

Education_____

Example Education:

B. Sc., Finance (High Honors), University of California 2002

Your Name

The top section, which features your name, address and contact information is self-explanatory. Make sure that the phone number you provide has voicemail, and as we discussed in the last section, this should ideally be a mobile phone number that is yours alone. As far as email addresses go, please make sure to use one that seems professional. I've seen email addresses on resumes that contained phrases like "Big Dog," "Sexy Peaches" and "Girls Love Me." These emails addresses are fine for communicating with (and amusing) your friends, but they will present an obstacle when they're put in print for a future employer to see. If you only have one email address and it contains a phrase like that, you can set up a new one for free that is more professional sounding. Use your name or some variation thereof. It will only take ten minutes and it can make the difference between getting called in for an interview and having your resume thrown in the trash.

Objective or Summary

This is the section that describes the value you'd bring to a prospective employer. As with all of the elements on your resume, a poorly written objective or summary can eliminate you from consideration right off the bat. Have a strong, well-written objective that will convey your enthusiasm, professionalism and skill level. It should also be tailored to the position you're applying for and not be too generic. You want to make sure that it doesn't just focus on you but it focuses on the employer and their requirements as well. I'm going to illustrate the differences between a strong, well-written objective statement and a poorly written one.

Bad, Job Seeker Focused: I want a finance position in a finance company that can utilize my 10 years of experience and lead me to a management role.

Good, Employer Focused: Finance professional with 10 years of experience in banking and accounting firms. Highly skilled in working across different departments, gathering cost-related data and providing senior executives with financial cost modeling reports.

The bad objective statement has everything you must avoid. It merely quantifies his years of experience without giving the prospective employer some tangible description of what he learned in his position or the skills he has demonstrated or developed in those ten years. It's generic and focused on himself. He states a career ambition but doesn't express how that goal is useful to the company he's applying to.

The good objective statement offers a lot of specific information about how he's served his previous employer well. He's highlighted skills and experiences that pertain to the position he's seeking. It's very targeted. **If you focus on your prospective employer's requirements and what you can offer them in your objective statement, you will naturally appeal to them more.** It all boils down to expressing what you can do for them.

Professional Experience

This section should be clear and well organized, just like the rest of your resume. Start with your most recent job and move backwards in chronological order. For the description of each position, you want to use compelling action words. You must reflect your skills and knowledge. It's also important to be specific and use percentages and numbers wherever possible. Here are two examples of how job seekers convey their professional experience on paper:

Bad: Job Seeker Focused:

- I am a financial expert

- I know how to work with all levels of management

- I am a good team member

- I am a good boss

Good: Employer focused:

- Delivered cost savings of 10% through financial cost modeling.

- Managed a team of 5 junior level financial managers who all exceeded their targets for the year and received promotions

- Facilitated critical senior executive level decision making through provision of financial cost modeling reports

The bad professional description is all focused on the job seeker and has nothing to do with the employer. The good description has percentages and numbers. It also begins with each bullet point with a strong action verb: "delivered," "managed," and "facilitated." Key words are also crucial. In this case, the key phrases used by this job seeker are "financial cost modeling" and "cost modeling reports." Key words aren't just important for when your resume is read. They can determine if your resume is read at all. When a recruiter receives a thousand resumes, he or she will search all of the resumes for ones that have a certain type of experience or contain a specific phrase. For this example, let's assume the hirer is looking for someone who has done financial cost modeling. The person hiring can do a computer search for the phrase "financial cost modeling" in all of the resumes and delete all those that don't contain that phrase without even looking at a single resume.

This job seeker also included specific numbers and percentages in the previous job description, which gives the employer a specific idea of what that last position was like. If the resume is written well, it can make the heart of the recruiter reading it race with excitement! In the above sample resume, we listed three positions. If you have been in the work force for twenty or more years, you don't need to include every job in that period. You should limit yourself to the last three or four that were critical.

Relevant Skills

"Relevant skills" refers to exactly that. What skills would be relevant for this position? For a financial position, our candidate would likely include their computer knowledge, such as Microsoft Excel and any other software he has experience with.

Education

This section is also pretty clear. If you are a recent college graduate and have minimal work experience, I recommend moving it to the top of your resume, just below the objective section. If it's been a few years or more since you've finished college, then it's best to put it down at the bottom. Also, the proper format if you have any graduate degrees is to list your highest degree first. If the person in the sample resume had an advanced degree, an MBA for an example, we would put that above their bachelor's degree so it would look like this:

Education_____

M.B.A., University of California Los Angeles 2005

B.Sc., Finance (High Honors), University of California 2002

There's no need to list anything prior to your bachelor's degree. If you didn't attend any schooling beyond high school, then list the high school you graduated from here.

In the next section, we'll get into the other type of resume I mentioned, the Functional resume.

Functional Resume

The other type of resume, the **functional resume**, is a lot less common than the chronological resume, but it's great for those trying to change careers or who recently graduated from school and don't have much or any experience.

If you're looking outside of your previous field, which may be customer service for example, the most impressive chronological resume in customer service won't be helpful when you're applying for a job in finance. A functional resume has the advantage of highlighting your skills with regard to how they would pertain to the job you're applying for. On the next page, I've provided an example of a functional resume, which we'll discuss.

Your Name

Street Address · City, State or Province

Phone Number · e-mail address

OBJECTIVE or SUMMARY

A resume Objective or Summary can help describe the value you bring to a prospective employer and entice a hiring manager to read your resume.

SKILLS SUMMARY

- Six years experience as an office assistant supporting two senior managers in Finance and Marketing
- Exceptional computer knowledge for analyzing reports in Excel and for building PowerPoint presentations
- Experience with coordinating meetings within various financial departments

SKILLS and EXPERIENCE

Financial Experience

- Led the development of financial cost models including the calculations of NPV values thus helping drive a 10% cost savings across the business unit.

SKILL GROUP TITLE

- Action words + Keywords + Skills + Knowledge
- Be specific using numbers and percentages

SKILL GROUP TITLE

- Action words + Keywords + Skills + Knowledge
- Be specific using numbers and percentages

EDUCATION

- Example Education: B. Sc., Finance (High Honors), University of Denver 2010 Metro College, 2002-2004,

Liberal Arts

- Continuing Education classes in: Microsoft Excel, Accounting, and Taxes Fundamentals.

Name

The top portion is the same as the other resume. As an aside, I should note that I've been astonished to see people forget to include their name or phone number. I assume errors like these are due to job hunter fatigue, so even if you're saying to yourself, "I would never make a mistake like that," do yourself a favor and have your partner or friend look at your resume to make sure there aren't any errors.

Skills Summary

This section, like all of the others, is designed to pertain to the employer and the job you are applying for. Don't mention your skills in carpentry if you're seeking a financial job. Your knowledge of Excel and PowerPoint is the type of information that would be relevant to this position.

Under the "Skills and Experience" section, the same rules from the chronological resume apply here as well. Be certain to use keywords, numbers and percentages to give your employer a clear idea of what your experiences consist of. The need for action words is also the same here.

Education

In the case of our applicant, we can see the need for the functional resume. He's a recent college graduate and he's trying to make a career change. Recruiters and HR professionals understand functional resumes. They recognize them instantly and will understand where you're going with them. There's absolutely nothing wrong with using a functional resume. Ultimately, a functional and a chronological resume both do the same thing: they provide a narrative of how you'll use what you know for the employer.

Resume Review

To conclude, I just want to emphasize how important it is to avoid being generic with your resume. Depending on how many different types of jobs you're applying for, you may need to have several different versions of your resume. Avoid any typos, and make your resume show how your experience applies to the job for which you're applying. You only have a minute or two to grab an employer's attention, so create an objective statement that will grab them.

Cover Letter

A well-written, enticing cover letter can get you even farther with a strong resume. It's an important calling card for you. If your cover letter underwhelms an employer, they will probably ignore your resume altogether. So don't let a good job slip through your fingers because of a sub-par cover letter. You should always send a cover letter with your resume. Don't make your reader try to figure out why you sent them your resume.

The first thing your cover letter should do is explain why you're applying for the job. Be specific when you contact the prospective employer. Do you want an internship, a summer position or a permanent position? Are you inquiring about a position upon graduation or a future employment situation? Let them know specifically why you're contacting them.

The next piece of information your cover letter should have is to let them know how you learned about the position and the company. Let them know if it was via a job posting on a bulletin board, a website, or a family member or friend who works at the organization. If you know someone who works for the company and mentioned the position to you, it's always a good idea to mention that person in the cover letter. That will help you get a leg up in the application process.

The next item you should address in your cover letter is to say what you would do for the company if hired. This part is vital. Remember, they don't really care about your experience or credentials or ability to impress, but about how you will help the company achieve their goals. You should mention what specifically you would help them with and also give them an analysis of their competitors.

I'll explain what I mean by that last part. A client of mine, Bill, applied for a position as a clerk at a hardware store. He had done his competitive analysis and knew what the competitors charged for their stock. In his cover letter, he recommended items that could improve their sales just based on his competitive research. Based on the information he provided in his cover letter, Bill was hired as an assistant manager even though he'd only applied for a clerk position! He was able to cull his information in one day by comparing prices at the competing hardware stores in the area. That one day increased his income and chances for future opportunities by getting him hired in a position above the one he inquired about. Going the extra mile will set you apart from the rest and allow you to start in a much higher position.

Your cover letter should also convince the reader to read your resume. To that end, your cover letter shouldn't be generic and should have specific references to the company you're applying for. Take the time to make this a persuasive document and it will pay off for you.

Also, highlight relevant areas of your background. Discuss specific areas of your own experience, education or expertise that will make you an ideal candidate for this position. Give them examples.

The writing style is important. Your cover letter should be written in your own style. People often use a style that is stiff or too plain, or simply not them. If you write in a style that isn't yours, you will seem inauthentic. If you express yourself in a way that is truly you, your letter will read as much more believable and will convey your enthusiasm convincingly.

You should also address gaps in your resume and provide any information that is specifically requested in the job ad. For example, if they request your availability date in the ad, let them know when you can start in your cover letter.

Another item your cover letter should address is to indicate when and how you will follow up with them. If you have the company's contact information, and nothing in the ad says "no phone calls," you should take the initiative and place a follow up call with the employer. A simple statement like this on your cover letter would be appropriate: "I will call you within the next week to see if you need any additional information from me." Don't assume they will contact you.

The last item, which differs from how a lot of people approach their application process, is to include a professional headshot photograph of you. I recommend a photograph of you smiling, looking directly into the camera. This will get you really noticed. If you're a recruiter and you're looking at a hundred resumes a day, don't you think a resume with a photograph would make you stand out? Especially if you've followed all of the other instructions for your cover letter and include a photograph, this will get you an interview even without them seeing your resume. (But definitely still include it!) I recommend that you smile in the photo. A smile is a universal symbol of warmth. If you have a straight face, people won't know how to read it and you make even seem upset.

So in conclusion, if you remember to follow all of these tips in your cover letter, or even if you just follow most of them, you will make a positive impression. Once you've demonstrated your intelligence and capability, you'll be far more likely to be asked to come in for an interview.

Video

Making an introduction video is optional, but I highly advise it. Immediately you will establish yourself as someone who is both creative and tech savvy. You can quickly give your prospective employer a chance to see you, hear you and connect with you. It sets you apart from the rest. If used effectively, the introductory video alone can get you an interview.

Ron, a client of mine, used an introductory video to apply for a job at a textile company. They were instantly impressed that someone who looked old enough to be their father had the technical wherewithal to create such a thing. His video indicated that they would be getting an experienced professional who was still open to new ideas.

Use your video as a chance to tell your employer what you would do for them, just as you would in your resume or cover letter.

The mechanics of making a video like this are relatively simple. Almost all digital cameras, smart phones and laptops can record video nowadays. There are free video hosting platforms like YouTube and Vimeo, which are very user-friendly too. After you've uploaded it, you can copy and paste the link to your video into an email or in the body of your cover letter. Be certain to keep your video brief, about three to six minutes long. In the video, make all of the points you would in a cover letter. Look into the camera, talk naturally and your personality will shine through.

Again, it's a very effective and original strategy. If you can include video, I definitely recommend it.

Recommendation Letters

Recommendation letters are something that most job seekers neglect to include. It doesn't just have to be from a former work supervisor. It can be from a local political figure, a minister at your church, or any prominent person who knows you. Use recommendation letters whenever possible. They speak volumes.

One of my clients, Susan, asked her former boss for a recommendation letter. She was happy he obliged, but disappointed when she read the actual content of it. Amid the compliments was the statement that she was sometimes difficult to work with. He added that overall she was a great team player and contributor to the workplace, but Susan didn't want to use the letter.

When she discussed it with me, I actually encouraged her to use it. This one negative comment lent greater credibility to all of the other positive statements in her letter. It was more believable than an overly glossy recommendation that would seem too good to be true. I told her that by sharing it with a prospective employer they would be more inclined to believe the other two glowing recommendations she had.

Susan got the job. After she was hired, she discussed the recommendation with her new boss. He told her that in his eleven years of hiring people, that was the most honest anyone had ever been in applying for a position at the company. Obviously, I only advise you to include a recommendation with a negative comment if the sum total of the letter is a positive assessment of you. If it's negative overall, throw it in the trash!

Always include a recommendation with your application, and if possible provide 2 or 3 recommendation letters.

If you have any award letters, include those too along with

your cover letter, resume, recommendations, and your video. This will constitute your application packet. It may be a bit time consuming, but the effort you spend up front will separate you from the rest.

Other Things To Do

There are other critical things that you need to do in addition to your resume, cover letter, video and recommendations. These are the last little things can make a critical difference.

First, set up and/or clean up your online profiles. In this era, social media can create an impression of who you are before you ever meet anyone at the company you're applying to. Set your Facebook profile and Twitter feed to private, along with any other social media site that isn't work-related. Employers do check you out online these days.

I've been face to face with clients and checked their Facebook profiles with them right there. It's a moment of clarity for many of them. One woman I was coaching had a photo of her in a very compromising position at a bachelorette party pop up as the first thing when I looked for her on Facebook. She realized that just wouldn't fly for type the position she was seeking.

If you don't have a social networking profile, I recommend getting started with LinkedIn or one of the other professionally geared social media sites. It's basically the same as having your resume online.

This next item may seem pretty obvious, but I want to emphasize that you must always have internet and phone access. I know some of you are in extremely hard financial situations, but it's vital to always be reachable for a last minute interview. There are pay-as-you-go cell phone plans for as little as $20 per month, which can make the difference between getting hired and remaining unemployed.

One of my clients only checked his email once a week when he was looking for a job. He lost two interviews because he didn't check his email in a timely fashion. If you don't have internet access, you can use free internet at the public library.

But having said that, I advise my clients to check their email 3 or 4 times per day. If an employer contacts 5 to 10 qualified people for an interview, they'll proceed with interviewing the ones who replied immediately and not worry about circling back to make sure the ones they didn't hear from come in.

Another key item is to always have your appropriate interview attire ready. Your suit or other professional outfit should be dry-cleaned and ready to be worn at a moment's notice for those last-minute interviews. It will help establish your own mental readiness too. Maintain your appearance with respect to shaving frequently and regular haircuts.

Lastly, I advise you to register on at least 2 job sites that are targeted to your industry. Most of these sites are free, although setting up your new account may initially be a little time consuming. Regardless, they are well worth the time spent. There are more general sites like Monster.com, but you can do a Google search to find sites that target your particular industry. Believe it or not, employers do go on those sites to do a keyword search in the hope of finding the right candidate for them.

Again, these are all matters that can come back to bite you so please do everything in your power to follow my instructions. Keep your social media presence clean and professional (or at least set to private); maintain your phone and internet access; keep an interview outfit ready at all times; maintain a professional appearance no matter how long you've been looking for a job; and don't forget to maintain a presence on at least two employment websites.

Getting Started Overview

I've given you a great deal of information in the preceding pages, so I recommend you use this section as a resource to refer to as needed. Your overarching task list for getting ready to interview should include these items:

- Create or update your resume

- Create your cover letter

- Video introduction (optional but very effective and highly recommended)

- Get recommendation and award letters

- Take care of other important details (dry-cleaned suit, haircut, social media and job hunting websites)

Now that you've done all of these things, you are truly ready to go on to the next step and start applying for the job of your dreams!

Applying For Jobs Online

It's time for some candor: a lot of people will take what they've learned so far about getting ready to apply for a job, and either due to feeling overwhelmed or thinking that they now have everything figured out, they will disappear. They'll stop reading this book, exit the conference room or miss the next workshop if it's at one of my live seminars. They will stop watching the training videos on HelpingFeet.com if they are studying my Job Getting System online

Significantly, what you have demonstrated by reading this far and continually showing up for this Job Getting System is that **you are determined and unstoppable**. So, you can drop any lingering doubts you have that this will not work for you. Congratulations and welcome to the next phase.

Applying for jobs online is one of the most popular methods used these days. I'll walk you through the steps of applying for jobs online in an easy to use and methodical way. Online job boards make it very easy for lazy people to apply for jobs just to see if they get a response. This has become a big problem. If you're a recruiter and you're trying to fill a specific position, you have to sift through thousands of resumes, many from people who might not even be interested in the position. So while online job boards are helpful, offering a great amount of data, they also present a problem. They attract everyone from out of the woodwork to apply for one position. In the pre-internet era, job boards were essentially the classified ads in your local newspaper. Now anyone in the world with internet access can find a help wanted ad and apply for a position.

Let's take a look at some of the job boards. There's Monster.com, CareerBuilder.com, Dice.com, HotJobs.com, as well as some job search engines like SimplyHired.com and Indeed.com. There are also some websites that are geared toward executive level positions, as well as many regional and country specific job boards depending on where you live in the world. Now, if you're looking for job boards in your specific field, those websites are just one Google search away. Bear in mind that the competition is enormous when you apply via a website. But I will give you numerous tools to help you stand out.

In this section, we will discuss:

- **The law of averages (36/12/6/2)**

- **Searching only for jobs you desire**

- **Researching your prospective employer**

- **Targeting your resume and cover letter**

- **Video recording (optional but recommended)**

- **How to apply**

- **Following up**

This will be an extremely detailed section, which will help you discover how to break through the online application process, which many of my clients have found impenetrable. But that is all about to change for you!

The Law Of Averages

Let's start by talking about my favorite law, the law of averages. Note: **A law affects you whether you believe it or not**. For example, it doesn't matter whether or not you believe in the law of gravity: if you are holding a book and you open your hand and release the book, the book you're holding will fall to the ground. It falls to the ground based on the law of gravity.

The Law of Averages is equally unassailable. I will show you how you can use it to get the job you really desire. So, let us talk about the law of Averages.

The Law of Averages is a universal law of nature. It does not err. The Law of Averages states that as the number of your trials for something increases, your chances of success also increase. For example, if you work out every day to lose weight, your chances of losing weight will increase. The same applies for job applications. If you apply for a job every day, your chances for getting a job increase. A lot of successful people who are in sales know about this law and they use it for their advantage. **Remember, you are in sales too. You are basically selling your time for money when you apply for a job.** Therefore, you can essentially use the law of averages to find a job or achieve anything else you want to in life.

36/12/6/2

The law of averages as it pertains to job seeking is this: If you send out 36 applications for 36 different positions, you will receive at least 12 replies. Out of those 12 replies, you will get 6 interviews. From those 6 interviews, you will get two job offers. This is the law of averages for your job search.

Now, if you're really good at applying for jobs using the system I've laid out for you, you may average a higher return rate of replies, interviews, and job offers. But by and large, 36/12/6/2 is the numerical rate for the Law of Averages of your job search. This is great news for you. By applying the methods I've outlined, you'll be able to plot out your plan for success.

Search For Only The Type Of Jobs You Desire

If I can facilitate only one change in your job search, it is that you only apply for the type of jobs you desire. This is the greatest gift you can give yourself. When you are pursuing work you truly desire, your enthusiasm and willingness increases tenfold.

This isn't just an abstraction. I'll give you an example from my own personal experience. I once applied for a job that had me managing processes and systems. I would have no interactions with people. I love people and I love jobs that at least have me interacting with people inside of the organization or, if possible, externally. So what was I doing even interviewing for such a position? Of course I did badly in the interview. The interviewer could see it on my face that I was totally uninterested in the job. He even tried to psych me up for it by pointing out the nice salary and benefits available for the position. In hindsight, it was a blessing in disguise that I did not get the job. I would have been completely miserable in the position. I use this example to illustrate that there is no point in pursuing a job that you don't want. This will help you avoid what is popularly know as the "job winner's curse" that is when you get a job that you don't really want.

We come to this place where we are willing to do something we hate out of desperation. We also have lost sight of the reality that there are literally thousands of jobs in areas that excite and interest us. It takes courage, but this is absolutely the right time to go after a job that you really want.

3 Applications Per Day

Once you've identified the type of job you really want, send out a minimum of three applications per day. Do this whether you feel like it or not. I've seen this with certain clients, who will only keep up their application process when they feel like it. Remember, you can always use the law of averages as a motivating factor to get past your feelings of not wanting to apply for a job on any particular day. If you can do more, great! But 3 is the barest minimum that you have to stick to in order to get a job within 30 days.

Research

Research is a vital way of establishing that you are a knowledgeable candidate. If you are contacted for a job by a recruiter, by all means ask them about the employer and the position. Otherwise, you can easily research the company you're applying to online. You can visit their website, their Facebook page, their Twitter feed, or any other information about them that's available online. When you visit their website, check out their "about us" page and their mission statement. This will also let you know if this is a place where you really want to work. You're going to be spending at least 40 hours per week with them, so get as much information about them as possible to decide if they're really right for you.

One of my clients was very conservative. He dressed in a suit and tie and liked working in places that were very structured. He applied to a laid back company that had no dress code and downplayed formality. Some of the employees even brought their dogs to work. I wondered how he would fit in at such a place. He didn't know either because he hadn't taken the time to research the company in advance of his interview. He had wasted his time because even if he'd somehow gotten hired, he would not have fit in there and probably would have been unhappy.

Call The Company

In the internet era, people have forgotten to use the phone. Calling a company is a great way to see if there is a job available there. Or, if you already know about a job opening there, you should call the company to ask them about the position. In the event that there's a position available, you can ask the person you speak to about all of the pertinent information. Get the name and email address of the person in charge of hiring, because the last thing you want to do is misspell the name of someone you'd like to work for. People may even have unique spellings for common first names. Write down the information they give you and repeat it back to them just to be 100% certain.

Research Their Competitors

We've already discussed the merits of researching the competitors of a company you're applying to. I'll give you another example that will illustrate why this is a good idea. Luis was a client of mine who wanted to apply to a local bakery. He identified and researched all the other bakeries in the area. Luis noticed that the bakery he was applying to had the lowest prices amongst the bakeries he'd researched. In his cover letter he suggested that the bakery increase their prices by 10%, which would still keep them below the prices the other bakeries were charging. This research only took about two hours in between calling and writing the cover letter. Guess what? He was hired without even interviewing for the position and was actually given a position higher in pay than the one he'd applied for. They were so impressed that anyone – let alone someone who wasn't an employee – had done a fact-finding mission like this. It indicated to them that Luis stood out from the crowd and was willing to go the extra mile.

Target Your Resume

Targeting your resume to the job for which you are applying is an absolute necessity if you want to convince an employer that you're the right candidate for the job. By making sure that you've included all of the relevant experience and key words, you can tremendously increase the odds that the hiring manager will look at your resume.

When you apply for a position, you should highlight the skills that pertain to the job in a different color. (Yes, I mean "highlight" in the literal sense.) Say for example that you're applying for a position where they want someone who has good customer service experience, communication skills, and an ability to do PowerPoint presentations. Assuming you have all of those skills, make certain to include those items in your resume, highlighted in a different color. When the person who has received the resumes electronically is sorting through them, your use of the relevant key words will make sure that they don't delete yours.

Also, reposition the most relevant skills to the top of your resume. You only have 30 seconds (if that) for your resume to grab the attention of the hiring manager, so make them count. A client of mine graduated from Harvard, but in order to find that out, someone looking at his resume would have had to scroll down to the bottom, where it was buried. I told him to move his education up to the top of his resume, so a recruiter would see that first. That's an extreme example, but in his case it was his biggest selling point. Use *your* resume as a way to emphasize *your* strongest selling points.

As we've already discussed previously, make sure your resume has no typos. Use spell check and have a friend proofread it as well.

In the course of this search, you'll be targeting your resume for each position you're applying for. I recommend saving each revised resume with the name of the company in the title of the document. For example, if your name is John Smith and you've applied to IBM, save your resume as "John Smith Resume_IBM." In the likelihood that you get called in for an interview, you can easily locate the resume you've sent in. You can make certain that you and the person interviewing you won't be discussing two different resumes.

Target Your Cover Letter

As with your resume, you'll want to update your cover letter to target each job's specific requirements. You'll want to mention all of the important information we discussed in the previous section: how you learned about the company and the position; which position you're applying for; address any gaps in your resume; and indicate how you will follow up. Also, I advise that you include a professional headshot photo with you smiling (even though some disagree with this tactic). It makes your whole resume and application packet stand out.

Record Your Video (Optional)

Recording your video is even more impactful than a headshot. Even if you're not highly tech savvy, this step is easily doable. You can simply sit in front of your laptop, most of which have video cameras nowadays, and record an introductory video at your desk. Be sure to keep it brief, about 3 to 6 minutes, and express to your prospective employer why you're an ideal fit for the position for which you're applying.

If you're intimidated by the technological element of making a video, you can enlist the help of a friend. You can upload it to Vimeo or YouTube for free and send the link to the person you'd like to work for. For those concerned about privacy, you can make the video password-protected or private so only the person you want to see it will. This should be a simple process and you can record it on a smart phone or tablet too. There's no need to get elaborate and hire a videographer. This is just an opportunity for you to speak directly to the person you want to hire you.

So again, while it is optional, I highly recommend it.

Applying

There are a variety of ways to apply for a job online. I'll walk you through each of them and give you some inside information that will help you stand out.

- Complete an online application form

- Email resume

- Fax over your resume and cover letter

- Send resume by mail

- Send resume by courier services (optional)

- Drop off your resume in person

Many people balk at the idea of sending an email by regular mail, but the fact that it's become less common will make your application packet stand out. They'll be much more likely to open mail versus an email resume, which they can promptly delete. Giving a hiring manager the experience of actually holding your application packet as a physical object makes it much harder for them to ignore it. Faxing your resume is a worthwhile approach for the same reason. For higher-level executive positions, sending your resume via FedEx, UPS, or the other courier services out there can help you distinguish yourself from the other applicants.

Dropping off your resume in person is also a strong approach that will get you noticed. This is especially valuable in service positions. If you do this, I recommend going in mid-morning, when the person doing the hiring is most likely to have an available minute to speak to you. This time of day is best because you've given them a chance to have their coffee and get settled. Later in the day is less desirable because by then people are tired and just want to go home. Try to hand your resume to the hiring manager personally, as opposed to handing it off to a receptionist. This will give you a chance to introduce yourself and show them how professionally you can represent yourself and their company.

Try to use two or three of these methods per job. There's no harm in that, unless of course their ad specifically states that they only want you to apply online. Otherwise, it's a chance to employ your newly acquired sales techniques to sell them your time for their money.

Following Up

You've given your prospective employer your polished, professional application packet and now it's time for you to follow up. This is where a lot of people drop the ball. A lot of people behave passively at this point and just expect to be called. Remember, you're competing with a lot of people so it's up to you to take the initiative. If, for example, the hiring manager wasn't available when you dropped off the application packet, take it upon yourself to call them and verify that they did receive it. A simple, polite two-minute phone call is all it takes. Unless of course they'd like more time to talk to you about the job, which is possible given the persistence you've displayed.

The follow-up is also a good time to respond to any of their requests for more information. They may want your work eligibility documents, references, or some other forms that must be completed. Most following up can be broken down into these categories:

- Responding to any request for information

- Form Filing

- References

- Criminal Background & Drug Test

- Signing of Non-Disclosure Agreements (NDAs)

A lot of companies will want you to pass a background check and a drug test as a condition of your employment. Many companies will also request a credit check, especially if the job you're being considered for involves being responsible for company money. At the executive level, non-disclosure agreements (NDAs) are becoming the norm. In some cases they will request that you sign an NDA just to interview.

Whatever is being requested or required of you, be certain to follow up right away. There are numerous candidates for the position you're seeking and you don't want to lose out because you hesitated.

Summary

We've covered a lot of material in this section, so I just want to briefly review what we've discussed before we move on to the next part.

- **The law of averages (36/12/6/2)**

- **Searching for only jobs you desire**

- **Researching prospective employer**

- **Targeting your resume and cover letter**

- **Video recording (optional)**

- **Applying**

- **Following up**

Among these items, the most foundational is that you target your resume and cover letter. It's great to practice all the other steps, but putting your energy and efforts at getting people to see a resume and cover letter that are generic will defeat the whole purpose. Revising your resume and cover letter to target a specific job will improve your chances exponentially.

Applying For Jobs Through Employment Agencies

I don't recommend employment agencies with much enthusiasm, but in some instances they can be useful. I just caution job seekers to only work with an employment agency that's reputable and has a proven track record of aiding job seekers successfully. There used to be only a few large employment agencies but now there are thousands whose sole purpose is to make money off of you while doing next to nothing. Most of these fly-by-night agencies just email a batch of resumes to an employer without much thought.

Employment agencies make money off of you by receiving a fee when you get hired. Therefore they're supposed to help you by coaching you and getting you ready for the interview process. Unfortunately, this is mostly unheard of nowadays. Most of the agencies in business now are lazy and greedy. A lot of job applicants don't realize they can ask for a consultation on your resume or interview coaching. These are ways that you can get them to earn their pay. The full list is here:

What Employment Agencies Should Do For You

- **Resume Review**
- **Research Potential Employer**
- **Research Hiring Manager**
- **Deliver Your Resume Packet**
- **Follow Up With Potential Employer For You**
- **Negotiate Your Pay**
- **Make Sure Your Employment Agency Earns Their Pay**

The best thing about employment agencies is that they are often privy to information about your prospective employer or hiring manager that may not be readily available to you personally. If they're a well-connected agency, they should be able to offer these types of insights. The employment agency should also be able to deliver your resume packet, including your cover letter, headshot photo, and video to the right hiring person at your potential employer's location. They are great for that.

Lastly, they can help you negotiate your pay. The employment agency ought to be well aware of what your position tends to pay and what competitive salary ranges are in your region and field. As I said, your employment agency makes money off of you by getting a fee for when you are hired. You may as well have them earn their keep.

Applying For Jobs Through Referrals

Most people think that applying for a job through a referral is as simple as asking a friend or family member to recommend you where they work. It's more involved than that when you do it effectively. This section will show you the art and science of how to properly maximize the advantage of applying for a job via a referral.

I'll give you an example of what typically happens when an applicant seeks a job through a referral. In this example, Jim is looking for a job. His friend Alan works at a company where Jim would like to work. Jim calls Alan and asks him if he knows of any job openings. Alan replies the way that a lot of people do who find themselves in this position. He's busy at work when he receives Jim's call, so he says the usual: "I don't think so but I'll ask around and get back to you." Most likely, that's the last time the subject will come up between the two friends.

Let's analyze this interaction on an emotional level. What's really happening here is that Alan regards Jim as a casualty and probably feels sorry for him. But a part of him may feel superior to Jim in some ways. Jim, on the other hand, subconsciously feels that he is better than Alan and resents the fact that Jim is the one who's working. There is also some resentment at that Alan can take care of his bills and his loved ones while Jim is still struggling.

Now with that emotionally fraught dynamic underlying their phone conversation, what do you think the results would be of Jim's inquiry? If you say, "probably nothing," you're correct. For Alan to help Jim, Jim will have to behave in a very different manner.

Do Your Homework First

The first thing Jim needs to do is research Alan's company and get any available information about specific job openings there. Jim should be pursuing the same process he would if he didn't know anyone who worked there: find out what the company is like via their website; visit their Facebook and Twitter pages to learn as much as possible about what they do and what working there would be like. Jim should decide in his research phase if this is a company that interests him before he contacts Alan.

Once Jim has done his research and decides that the company is a good fit for him, he should ask to meet with Alan. During that meeting, Jim should start by asking Alan about his job and about the company. Jim should let Alan speak first about what's going on with him and his career and not start by discussing his own needs. This is important because people like to talk about themselves. It will also give Jim an opportunity to demonstrate that he's a great listener.

After Jim has listened to Alan at length, it's his turn to ask for the referral. That's where the neuroscience of this approach comes in to play. It's an opportune time because Alan will feel obligated to help Jim after Jim has patiently listened to Alan speak at length. Of course, while Alan was talking, Jim wasn't just biding his time to ask for a favor. Without necessarily realizing it, Alan was imparting useful information about the company that Jim can use to target his application.

When asking for the referral, Jim also has a chance to ask for other pertinent information, focusing his questions only on the positions he's decided he's interested in. He can ask things like: Who is the hiring manager? What are that department's challenges? What is the company culture? And so on. If Alan doesn't know, Jim should politely ask if he could find out for him.

Once Jim has all the information he needs, he should proceed to the next step, which is to follow the company application process. Even if you have a personal contact, for large companies or governmental agencies, there is a specific application process that doesn't allow for any variance. Following their procedure is to your advantage and can also help the person who referred you. Many companies actually offer a bonus to employees who refer the applicants they hire.

The next step is for Jim to hand over his application packet to Alan so that Alan can hand-deliver it to the hiring manager. By now you should know what the application packet includes, but I'm happy to enumerate the items included for those who forgot. The packet contains your resume, your cover letter, your references and award letters, your photo headshot, and, if you've recorded an introduction video, include a link to that as well or a CD/DVD copy of your recording. As we discussed previously, by applying through the company's designated application process, you're doing what all the other prospective employees are doing and you're not really standing out. But with Alan's help, Jim will get his application packet to the right person and will definitely stand out.

If for some reason Alan is unable to get it to the hiring manager - which may be the case if it's a large company and there are several locations – Alan can still send it to the hiring manager using the company's inter-office mailing system. Even though it's not a direct hand-off, this is still a much better situation than for Jim to mail in his application packet himself. First of all, inter-office mail is given greater priority than an envelope that comes in regular mail from someone that's a stranger to the hiring manager. Also, there is much more accountability to follow through on an application when it's received from a colleague.

Jim's ability to get Alan on his side and showing up with specific knowledge about the company and the position he wants totally transformed Jim and Alan's interaction. Also, Alan can continue to provide Jim with inside information during the interviewing process.

In summary, when you ask someone you know for a referral, be sure to take these steps:

- **Research the company**

- **Get as much information as possible from the person you want to refer you**

- **Then ask for the referral**

- **Follow the standard company application process**

- **Hand over your targeted resume packet to referral to hand-deliver for you**

And last but not least, show your appreciation to your referrer. Buy them dinner when you're celebrating your new job!

Applying For Jobs Through Career Fairs

So far, you've already amassed a strong arsenal of methods and skills for your job hunt. You are at a strong advantage compared to all of the other people out there who are applying for jobs. You've also demonstrated a great deal of determination by reading this far. When you apply that level of determination to your job search, it's only a matter of time before you get the job you truly desire.

The next area where you can improve your effectiveness is at job fairs. Job fairs are a great opportunity to meet recruiters and HR personnel from numerous companies and, if you work this process correctly, you can get an interview and even obtain a job offer all in one day.

While most people write off job fairs as an ineffective way of getting hired, you can definitely get a job from a career fair. Over 70% of human resources departments participate in and rely on job fairs to recruit their employees. They are not only a great event for looking for and applying for your next job, they are also an excellent way of expanding your professional network, gathering information about your industry, learning about new products and services, and collecting business cards of individuals you will follow up with later.

Niche career fairs, which cater to specific industries such as finance, retail, customer service and sales, are an excellent way to apply for jobs. I highly recommend attending niche career fairs over the more general ones, which will house all kinds of businesses under one roof. In fact, I encourage you to attend niche career fairs whenever you can.

As I said before, many job hunters have erroneously concluded that job fairs are a waste of time. But if you attend these events using the strategies I'm about to lay out for you here, they will be well worth your time.

Key Tips

Do your homework before you arrive. Find out in advance which employers will be at the event. Career fair organizers typically post that information on their website. If it's not available, don't be shy. Call the event organizers and ask them to email or fax you their list of participants. Once you have your list, go through it and highlight the companies you'd like to connect with.

Next, create a resume packet that's targeted for each company. If possible, apply in advance for any positions that interest you at those companies. When you're submitting that application, be sure to let them know that you will be at the career fair and you'll be available for an interview when you're there.

Arrive at the event early and get familiar with where the companies with whom you'd like to connect are situated. Give yourself plenty of time to get there early, so you don't start your day stressed out about finding the place or getting there on time. Getting there early also increases the likelihood that the representatives of the companies you're applying to will have the time and energy to interview you. Later in the day, after they've seen hundreds of people, they're just tired and blurry and won't be able to differentiate you from someone else. Early attendance also cuts down on the likelihood of having to wait in a long line to get into the event or speak to certain high profile employers. In the event that you do have to wait in a long line, simply use that as a chance to review your notes on the company so the facts you've prepared about them will be fresh in your mind when you talk to someone.

Be prepared when you show up to the event. Have extra paper and pens ready. In addition to your targeted resume packets, it's also important to have extra resumes for the companies that you hadn't targeted but still may pique your interest. Wear comfortable, professional looking shoes that you will be able to stand in for a long time. If the event has nametags, by all means, wear one. This is your chance to create a first impression, much like a job interview. Come dressed for success with professional attire. Smile often and continually tell yourself that you will get a job today.

When you meet people, greet them with a firm handshake. By this I don't mean an overpowering display of physical strength, which will turn people off. Use your handshake to display warmth and enthusiasm while smiling and making eye contact with the interviewer.

Be targeted in your conversations. Be concise, polite, and direct. You only have a brief window to get the information that you'd like and to show that you're the ideal candidate for them. **Don't ever ask them if they have any openings.** This is one of the worst things you could ask because it shows an obvious lack of targeting. I'll give you an example of what you should say to impress your interviewer and show your awareness of their company's needs.

Let's say that you meet a recruiter and notice that his nametag reads "John." This is how a targeted, effective introduction statement would sound: "Hi John. My name is Kate. I'm seeking the position of an account executive. I bring to the table extensive knowledge as an account executive that I would apply directly to this position if given the opportunity and here is how: I would use my five years of experience as an account executive to make sure that I deliver on my targeted sales goal for your company each and every month like I did with my previous employer. I met every single goal set for me each month for five years straight and will do the same for your organization. Also, I would leverage my network of previous clients and customers to deliver on your company's sales goals and hit the ground running from day one if given the opportunity."

If you're at the booth talking to an actual recruiter and not just a company rep, they will want to talk to you about your career objectives, strength, willingness to relocate if necessary, interests, and relevant skills for the type of job you desire. They would also want to find out from you why you want to work for their organization and how you would be an asset. So be ready to answer those types of interview questions, then provide them with your resume packet and *ask for a second interview*. That is if they haven't offered you one already. I can tell you from extensive experience that you are much more likely to be asked to come in for a second interview by telling them very specifically what you can do for them rather than telling them about yourself. Often times, they send people to career fairs who are not in the position to hire you. If that's the case, ask them who the hiring manager is, their contact information, and what the next steps are to getting a second interview. If a recruiter is not accepting resumes, ask them what their application process is.

Lastly, rinse and repeat. You'll want to go through all of these same steps I've described with each of the companies you've targeted. In bullet points, those steps are:

- **Do your homework before you arrive**

- **Arrive early and get familiar with location**

- **Be prepared**

- **Be targeted**

- **Rinse and repeat**

If you have extra time after connecting with the companies you've targeted, by all means stick around and talk to the other companies represented there. You never know what other discoveries you could make at an event like this.

Review

To conclude, I just want to reiterate the importance of using career fairs as a chance to speak to the actual person who does the hiring. If they're present at the career fair, excellent. If not, once you've impressed the company representative by clearly stating what you can do for them, ask for the hiring manager's name and contact information. This approach is far more effective than simply handing your resume to what I call a "resume collector" who will just add yours to a pile and forget about you. Your proactivity is what will make all the difference here.

Also, this is a very busy event, so be sure to take notes so you can keep the follow-up instructions from the various companies straight. I've found it best to jot down the next steps on the back of the recruiter's business card. If they don't have a business card, simply record all the relevant information in your notepad.

After you've talked to someone, be sure to thank him or her. Say "thank you" at the end of your conversation, but also follow-up with a thank you note. You will stand ahead of the vast majority of your competition, who for whatever reason, mostly do not write thank you notes. When you demonstrate that you can represent yourself so impeccably, they will want you to represent their company that way too.

Interviewing For Jobs On The Phone

In the last few sections, we looked at creative ways to apply for a job. Now we'll get into the details about how to interview for a job, starting with phone interviews. A phone interview usually precedes any other type of interview. So, in this section, we'll discuss what to do before, during and after your phone interview so that you'll be able to ace all of your phone interviews with ease and grace. You'll no longer feel the anxiety that can overpower some job seekers during the interview process.

Most employers nowadays use phone interviews as a preliminary screening process to narrow down the pool of job applicants, then moving on to the smaller selection that will be invited for the in-person job interview. The phone interviews have shifted from more casual in tone to a chance for employers and recruiters to pose very in-depth questions typically reserved for face-to-face interviews. In the past, phone interviews typically consisted of a few simple questions that most applicants could breeze through in ten minutes or less. They could generally expect to be asked in after the call. However, that's not the case anymore.

The bar has been raised for phone interviews. For some jobs, the phone interview decides if you can make it on to a *second* phone interview. Essentially, phone interviews nowadays require the same amount of preparation that in-person interviews do.

The big difference between a phone interview and an in-person interview is that over the phone you can't observe any of the interviewer's non-verbal cues, such as facial expressions or body language. But by using the tips I'm about to give you, your inability to see their reactions won't matter. Even over the phone, you'll undoubtedly demonstrate how well suited you are for the position and be asked back for an in-person interview. Remember that the main goal is to get an in-person interview from your phone interview. In the following pages I'll show you exactly how to do that with calmness and confidence.

What To Do Before The Interview

Unfortunately, gone are the days of "winging it" for a phone interview. Treat these interviews with the same level of attention and preparation you would a face-to-face interview.

While the interview is taking place, it will be immensely helpful for you to have the ad you replied to and your targeted resume and cover letter in front of you. Having that information at your fingertips will be helpful for any questions you'll need to answer. You should also have a list of your own accomplishments as they pertain to the job you're interviewing for in front of you.

In addition to those items, have your research you've done on the company in front of you. Being able to reference any information you know about the company during the interview will be extremely useful. I also recommend having your notes typed or written up in such a way that you can easily glean these facts while you're discussing them with your interviewer. If you type out your notes, I recommend a large font, double spacing, and having the facts you know you'll want to refer to in bold face. Or just use any method that works for you so you don't have to read through several densely written pages of your own research to find the information you want. You want to appear as off-the-cuff as possible.

Have a pen and paper ready. You will likely need to write down information – ideally the time and place for your follow-up face to face interview - and the last thing you want to do is ask an interviewer to wait while you find something to write with. It also helps to have your calendar there to schedule any subsequent appointments.

In general, make sure to clear your environment of any distractions while you're being interviewed. Ask your kids to play somewhere else and have them take the dog with them too. Turn off the TV, radio or any other electronic noise. If for some reason they call when you're not expecting it and you feel unprepared, you are well within your rights to ask to speak to them later. But you need to take the initiative and suggest a specific time later in the day, preferably within a couple of hours, or by the next day at the latest.

Ideally use a landline for this phone call, unless you're 100% confident in the quality and reception of your cell phone. Turn off your call waiting so you're not distracted during the interview. (If you're dialing the interviewer, you can dial *70 before entering their phone number to turn off call waiting if you are in the USA.) Your interviewer is very busy and will probably have little patience for a call disrupted by static or other disturbances.

In talking to my clients, I'm astonished by how many of them will have no questions for their interviewer. Nine times out of ten, when given the opportunity to ask any questions, interviewees will say they don't have any. This is exactly what you don't want to do. It reflects a lack of knowledge and interest about the company. But do be mindful of your interviewer's time and keep your list of questions brief: three to five is a good range.

Practice interviews are an excellent way of knowing how you come across during interviews. Have a helpful friend, spouse or trusted family member ask you some interview questions you expect to be asked and be sure to tape your answers. Listen to them later, even if you don't want to - *especially* if you don't want to! It's a chance for you to hear how you come across. All of those uh's, um's, pauses and use of the word "like" as a frequent digression are fairly common, but not very professional sounding. Be mindful of those habits when you do your actual interview.

Personally, interviewing on the phone is my favorite part of the process. It's the equivalent of an open-book test. I can have all of my information spread out in front of me to really give myself a leg up. By doing that as well as following these key steps, you will truly transform your interviewing process:

- **Have the job ad, the cover letter and the resume which you sent in response to the ad**

- **Have your research you've done on the company in front of you**

- **Have a pen and paper handy for note taking**

- **Clear the room**

- **Use a high quality phone**

- **Have a short list of questions about the job**

- **Practice interviewing**

So these are the key elements of preparation. But what are some ways of making yourself stand out during the phone interview? Keep reading to find out.

What To Do During The Phone Interview

So your prospective employer has called you at the time you were expecting and you're sitting at your desk with your resume, cover letter, the ad you replied to, and a handy cheat sheet of all your research laid out in front of you. The conversation is in progress, and here's what you're telling them: **"Here is what I would do for you if hired."** I've said this before in this book, but it's such an important message that it bears frequent repeating. Don't just tell them about what you know, which they don't care about, but about how you'll use that knowledge to help the employer achieve his or her goals. When you discuss your background, education, and past experience, it should be short and simple and kept in the realm of how it pertains to the job you're applying for.

Many people err in the above approach. They conclude that because of their prestigious education or prior positions, that should be sufficient to get them hired. This is one of the main reasons why so many people have a hard time getting a job. **They don't clearly specify what they will do for the employer with what they know.**

Be prepared to ask questions. Phone interviews, just like in-person interviews, are an opportune time to ask questions. The interview process is a two-way street. You need to make it clear why they would want you to work for them, but this is also a chance to determine if you'd like to work for them. But when I say you should ask questions, don't just ask questions about salary and benefits. Ask questions such as "what would be my day to day activity?" You want as much clarity as possible about what your experience there would be like.

Next, provide specific examples when you answer questions about your work history. General answers make for okay conversation but won't make you stand out. A good answer would follow this blueprint: "at my last job I had a specific problem related to 'X' and this is how I went about solving it."

When you're in conversation with your interviewer and providing examples, I want you to follow the **STAR Principle.** STAR is an acronym for **S**ituation, **T**ask, **A**chievement and **R**esults.

STAR Principle

Situation

- Briefly describe background information

Task

- Explain expectations/requirements or what had to be accomplished

Achievement/Action

- Detail your actions showcasing your skills – What you did

Result

- Indicate outcome and what your learned from the experience

The STAR Principle is based on the idea that previous behavior and action is the best indicator of future behavior and action. That's why it's to your advantage to answer each question by describing what you did in a certain situation and the ensuing results.

Here's an example of a response to a question and I'll show you how the STAR principle works. Let's assume they ask you the question, "Describe a situation where you had to work with a difficult employee."

Using the STAR principle, your reply would be something

along the lines of: "While I was a supervisor, I had an employee who was consistently 10 to 20 minutes late every day. I had a discussion with her in which I asked her what the reasons were for her lateness. She explained that after dropping her children off at school in the morning, her commute kept her from arriving on time. Upon mutual agreement, I adjusted her schedule, changing her hours from 9 to 5 to 9:30 to 5:30. She was never late again."

Here is how the STAR principle applies to the example I just gave. The situation is "While I was a supervisor, I had an employee who was consistently 10 to 20 minutes late every day."

The task is to address the issue with the employee constantly showing up late for work.

The action part of your example is "I had a discussion with her in which I asked her what the reasons were for her lateness."

The result part of this scenario is "She explained that after dropping her children off at school in the morning, her commute kept her from arriving on time. Upon mutual agreement, I adjusted her schedule, changing her hours from 9 to 5 to 9:30 to 5:30. She was never late again."

This situation, task, action and results formula for answering questions is the formula you should use for answering all of your questions about prior work experiences.

Other things I recommend are to always be polite and well spoken on the phone. Observe phone etiquette and smile while you're speaking, even though they can't see it. It's a classic phone sales technique and it actually changes the tone of your voice and the person at the other end of the call can hear it. Refer to someone as "Mr." or "Ms." unless they ask you to call them by their first name. Be mentally present for this conversation. I spoke to a recruiter who could tell that her interviewee was going through a fast-food drive thru while she was talking to him. Your cheeseburger can wait! Give your interviewer your undivided attention. Avoid smoking, eating, chewing gum, or drinking during your call.

Lastly, take your time with your answers. It's okay to take a brief pause before you answer a question to organize your thoughts. But do answer succinctly. Giving a long, disjointed answer will leave your interviewer confounded and less likely to ask you in for a face-to-face interview. If your answer is too short, don't worry. Your interviewer will ask an appropriate follow-up question.

Another technique I encourage is to stand or sit up straight when speaking to an interviewer on the phone. Your voice sounds more assertive in these positions than when slouched or lying down. One of my clients conducted an interview while lying in bed. This unorthodox location made him decide that it was just fine to speak to the female interviewer like a prospective girlfriend. The interviewer, to whom I'd recommended this client, called me after the interview totally horrified. Needless to say, the Don Juan approach didn't help my client get hired. Standing or sitting upright will also help minimize all of the uh's and um's we talked about before.

If your interviewer asks you what sort of salary you're seeking, you should never answer this question. You should deflect and reply with the honest answer, "At this point I'd need to learn more about the position to answer that accurately. I'd love to meet for a face-to-face interview to discuss the job further. I'd be able to give you a realistic answer once I know more about the position." Answering this way will establish a noticeable *lack* of desperation on your end and will also establish you as someone who is circumspect in their professional dealings.

So to review, by following all of the steps I've discussed, which I've listed in bullet form, you will easily proceed to either a second phone interview or an in-person interview. Just remember:

- **Tell them what you would do for them.**

- **Ask questions**

- **Provide examples (use the STAR Principle)**

- **Observe proper phone etiquette and smile**

- **Take your time**

Of course, your follow-up should be as professional and polished as your phone interview. We'll discuss that in the following section.

What To Do After The Interview

As you're wrapping up your phone interview, ask your interviewer if any of your responses were unclear. I did this once and the hiring manager said he was glad that I asked that, as one of my replies left him confused, but he opted not to pursue it. In fact, I found out that based on my earlier, unclear reply, he'd decided to pass me up for a second interview. But after I clarified my response, I was now his number one pick. Just asking one simple question moved me from last place to the number one prospect. Eventually, it also got me hired.

Before you hang up, you should also make a point of asking for the interviewer's email address and phone number if you don't already have it. The email is most important. The day of the interview, send the interviewer a thank-you note for their time in which you reiterate your interest.

While still on the phone, ask about the next steps of the hiring process. Be sure you have a clear idea of what their timeline is and who the decision makers are. Be careful here not to barrage them. A couple of simple questions to demonstrate your interest and enthusiasm should be enough. Let them know you're available if they have any follow-up questions as well.

At the end of the interview, give the interviewer a 90-second summary. Here is an example that touches on all of the important ideas you want to convey: "Thank you for giving me the opportunity to interview today for this position. I hope I have answered all of your questions to your satisfaction. If not, I can clarify them while we're still on the phone. I also want you to know that I would really love having the opportunity to use my experience and qualifications to add value to your organization. I'm available to answer any additional questions you might have afterwards. I look forward to the next step of the process. Thank you again for your time."

While the interview is still fresh in your mind – ideally as soon as you hang up the phone - take notes on what you were asked and how you answered it. Be as objective as possible, because if you don't receive an offer for a second interview, you can see if there's anything you could have said differently. Of course, if they do ask you in for a face-to-face interview, this can also be a useful record of what you said that impressed them.

- **Ask if any of your responses were unclear**

- **Get their email address and send a thank-you note that day**

- **Ask about the next steps**

- **Provide a 90 second summary**

- **Take notes about what you were asked and how you answered**

By applying all of these techniques, you will drastically increase your odds of getting that face-to-face interview you want and get hired.

Review

By now you've learned how to prepare for the phone interview and what to do during and after the interview. When the phone rings, just answer with a professional greeting by saying "Hello, this is Steve" or whatever your name is, and let the conversation unfold naturally. While you're looking for a job, answer any number you don't recognize as politely and professionally as possible. If you're caught off guard when they call for a phone interview or you're too busy to talk, ask them if you can call them back in a few minutes, or, if you're truly unable to talk to them, later that day or the following day. Any delay longer than that can count against you, as they're likely contacting many candidates.

Keep practicing your phone interview skills. You'll get better with each successive phone interview, especially if you've gotten in the habit of taking notes right after the interview so you'll notice your successes and where you have room to grow.

Just bear in mind these points:

Prepare before the interview and be diligent with your follow-up

Practice, practice, practice so the conversation flows naturally!

By applying enough preparation and honing your message of what you can do for your employer using what you know, you'll ace the phone interview and be ready to move on to the face-to-face interview! Keep reading for my inside pointers on how to ace that too.

Interviewing For Jobs In Person

In our last section, I outlined how to master the phone interview. Now that you've successfully done that, your prospective employer has asked you to come in for an interview. Or they were so impressed by your application packet that they asked you to come in for a sit-down interview without a phone interview. Either way, you're about to meet your next potential employer.

So now what? How do you ensure that you don't make any important missteps during the interview? That's what this section is for. In this section, I'm going to discuss how to overcome interview jitters and sail through any in person interview with flying colors.

Every company has their own way of conducting an interview. Some businesses do a panel-like interview, while others prefer one-on-one interviews. Generally you can expect to interview with two to four people, typically the people you will end up working with, including a group manager or department head. If it's a small business, it may even be the company owner. The entire interview process can go from one to six hours in the case of more senior-level executive positions. If the interview overlaps lunch hours, the company will typically provide lunch. You can expect a wide variety of questions that range from common personal questions to complex, detailed questions. Remember, the whole process is about the employer determining if you have the skills and knowledge that will help them achieve their goals. They also want to know if you're someone they would like to work with.

There are only two possible outcomes to the interview: you either get hired or you don't get hired. So don't make yourself unnecessarily anxious. It's not the end of the world if you get passed over. Just learn from it and move on to the next one. Most importantly, the number one quality for getting hired is to tell your employer what you can do for them. Let them know that you are smart and able to accomplish their goals.

What You Should Do Before The In-Person Interview

Just as you prepared before your phone interview, you need to do the appropriate preparations beforehand. In fact, you should ask your prospective employer as much as possible about the hiring process in advance of your sit-down interview. Ask how long the interview will take. If they indicate they'll be keeping you longer, that means they think you're a strong candidate and would like to speak to you at length. You should also find out how many people will be interviewing you and their roles within the organization. This is so you know how many resume packets to bring and who you'll be talking to. You can also do some research about these individuals in advance via social networking sites or the company website. Another question you can ask is what the timetable is for hiring the new employee, so you know when to check back in with them.

Be sure to research the company as much as possible. You need to be prepared to answer the question, "What do you know about our company," and especially, "Why do you want to work here?" Knowing about the company and their issues will enable you to be more interactive during the interview and give you an edge over the other applicants who may go to the interview with large gaps in their knowledge of the company.   Before the interview review the company's website. You should be looking for things like their key products and services; what do they sell; what is their corporate culture; how is the workplace environment; who are their competitors and chief suppliers; who are their customers; and recent changes and their impact. Don't be afraid to call your interviewer and ask for the company's literature too.

I can't emphasize how important it is to have a clear idea on what the company you're applying to does. I've had people show up to interviews that had the audacity to ask, "So what do you guys do?" That's probably the best way to end an interview on the spot.

You should also diligently prepare three to five questions. Starting your questions with qualifiers such as "Upon my research of your company, I noticed..." It's also helpful to have more than 5 questions prepared in the event that some of your questions get answered during the interview. You'll still want to have some questions ready to ask if they happened to address some of the questions you prepared. The odds of having all 5 questions answered during the interview are slim. Don't worry about needing to check your notes to see what questions you've written down. It will just make you look prepared. Studies have shown that asking your prospective employer questions makes you more likely to get hired. My only caveat is to avoid questions that aren't about salary, benefits, and vacation at this stage of the hiring process.

The next thing you'll want to do is mentally prepare. Remember that with a job you are basically selling your time for money, so be prepared to put your best foot forward. Just as a store manager does her best to display her merchandise in the most attractive manner, you should do the same. Put your most positive qualities on display while also using the interview as an opportunity to determine if this is someplace you'd like to work.

As for your attire, men should wear a suit and women should wear something formal. You are much better off being overdressed than underdressed. For women, avoid wearing anything too revealing or something that's more appropriate for a nightclub than an office. Be properly groomed. Show up clean-shaven or with your nails done, depending on your gender, and with your hair recently cut. Your personal appearance is very important. First impressions matter and people make quick conclusions about you based on that. Appearing dirty or unkempt may cost you the job.

During an interview I conducted years ago, I was part of a panel of three people interviewing a woman with an impeccable resume. When she showed up, it was as if she had bathed in her perfume. The odor was overpowering and we were enclosed in a small room. One of my fellow interviewers had asthma and he was actually having a hard time breathing. The other interviewer kept saying "it's kind of hot in here" as she was struggling to breathe. We wound up rushing through the interview in 15 minutes even though we'd allotted an hour to talk to her. We were so relieved to finally get rid of her that we could barely remember anything we'd talked about. Needless to say, we decided not to ask her back. So the rule is: no strong cologne or perfume. Better yet, just stick to deodorant.

Before you start your trip to the site of the interview, have your driving directions ready. Give yourself an extra fifteen minutes (at least) and find out in advance where you should park. Bring extra coins if you'll need to park at a meter.

Also, as with a phone interview, do plenty of practice interviewing. Tape your interview so you can gauge your performance, on video if possible. You want to convey a persona that is relaxed, composed, and capable. Be sure to have your friend ask you the types of questions you'd expect to be asked in the interview. You want to have answers ready instead of having to improvise when you're in front of someone who wants to possibly hire you.

The aforementioned steps will help guide the interview into a positive, relaxed process that will hopefully result in being offered the position. Here are the items we discussed in bullet form:

- **Get as much information as possible about the interview beforehand**

- **Research the company**

- **Prepare for the interview**

  - Prepare questions

  - Mentally prepare

  - Prepare your appearance

  - Have directions ready

- **Practice interviewing**

Now that we've established the foundation you'll lay during your preparation process, let's delve into exactly how to act during your interview.

During The In-Person Interview

During your in person interview, you'll want to use this as a platform to convey what you'll do for your employer. You'll spotlight your skills and experience as they pertain to the job you're seeking and the company's objectives. Reflect your well-researched knowledge of the company and communicate your interest to them. Discuss ways you have contributed to other organizations, your prior successes, and your career goals, which should be in line with your employer's.

If your plan is to work there for a year and then move on to some place preferable, keep that to yourself. An employer is not interested in training someone only to lose them to another employer or competitor. Even if that is your intention, you don't need to share that.

Finally, share examples with your interviewer of how you made things better in your last job by either leading a team or being an integral part of one. Be prepared to weave these items into the conversation so you can provide context, action, and the results you achieved. Remember the STAR Principle: Situation, Task, Actions and Results. That is where you provide examples of what you've done to demonstrate the job criteria. The STAR Principle is based on the idea that previous behavior and action is the best indicator of future behavior and action. (If you need an example of the STAR Principle, consult the last section on phone interviews.)

Again, asking questions in your interview is important. It shows your preparedness and interest in the company. When people demur, either out of a fear of "rocking the boat" or asking something they already ought to know, they are placing themselves behind the other candidates who have come with thoughtful questions. One trick I like to use is that I will ask questions that will allow the interviewer to talk about how great their company is or about themselves. Asking your interviewer why they like working there allows you to find out a lot about the company by getting the interviewer to go off script.

You'll want to be mindful of your body language and etiquette. Definitely don't chew gum, eat, drink anything besides water, or smoke. If you are a smoker, I recommend avoiding cigarettes until after your interview. Coming into an interview smelling of the cigarette you smoked on the way in can land your application in the reject pile. Smile often and mind your posture. Sit up straight, leaning forward slightly to show that you are engaged. It's also a good idea to take notes throughout, as this will indicate your interest. Smile when appropriate and make frequent eye contact with everyone in the room. Greet everyone with a handshake and a smile.

Remember to turn off or set your phone to silent before the interview, and under no conditions should you answer a call or text during the interview. Be confident that you have every reason to be there. Remember, they are interviewing you because you have impressed them.

Be sure to bring your resume packet that has your cover letter and references for everyone in the room, plus an extra copy for yourself.

Remember to keep the conversation professional. You don't need to bring up your personal life or any other outside issues. If you and the interviewer both discover you're fans of the same basketball team, great. But otherwise, don't instigate any topics that are outside the scope of a job interview. Also, if you find out your interviewer has political leanings you disagree with, you don't need to bring up your own affiliations. You don't want to disagree or be seen as opposite from your interviewer for any reason. Definitely steer clear of politics, religion or other polarizing topics. Don't use this as an opportunity to demonstrate your edgy sense of humor, either. They may not appreciate it or be in a laughing mood. Also remember to never bad-mouth your previous boss. And while I'm sure almost none of you would ever do this, absolutely never flirt with the interviewer. Steer clear of asking about money or vacation time or expressing your disdain for companies that stay open the week between Christmas and New Year's. Speak clearly and be sure to keep a glass of water on hand in case you get dry mouth. Remember to keep it formal, referring to people with "Mr." or "Ms." unless they tell you otherwise.

Remember, your goal is to set yourself up for a situation where they hire you. Anything that works against that objective is best left out of the interview.

Instead of being afraid during an interview, think of it as a controlled environment where you have a captive audience to convey how good a fit you are for this company. While interviews have historically been intimidating for many job seekers, they don't have to be. You have guidelines and your own mental checklist that will help propel you through the interview and, most likely, to getting a job offer. Just keep reminding yourself of these key ideas:

- **Again, tell them what you can do for them with examples**

- **Ask questions**

- **Watch your body language and etiquette**

- **Bring several copies of your resume**

- **Keep it professional**

Standard Interview Questions

While I can't give specific answers that will work for each of the people reading this book, there are a number of recurring questions interviewers ask. There are however proven guidelines that will help you answer in the most effective way possible. Here are my tips on how to answer some of the most common interview questions.

Tell me about yourself.

This is not the moment to tell them about your love of horses or the summer you spent in Colorado painting watercolors. What you want to do is tell them about your background as it pertains to the position you're applying for. Your answer isn't exactly about "yourself." It's about how you can provide value to that employer.

Why should we hire you?

This is you chance to let them know that you've already

performed for another employer the very same tasks you'd be performing at this job. You should also mention the point I've been instilling: explain what you will do for them using your knowledge and experience.

What are your strengths and weaknesses?

Use the STAR principle to describe your strengths and how you've used them in the past. For your weakness, you need to be careful. Don't volunteer anything that could potentially disqualify you. It's best to bring up a weakness that's actually tied to one of your strengths. When I've been asked this question, I have said that when I want to solve a problem, I become so determined to get it done that I will spend a lot of time trying to solve it immediately. By sharing that weakness, I've been up front with the interviewer but it's also something that reveals my diligence. You also need to explain how you've addressed that weakness. In the case of my need to solve a problem right away, I say that my way of addressing that is to check in with myself when I notice that I'm doing it and recalibrate my efforts so I don't wear myself out. I also mention that I've learned over the years not to put unnecessary effort toward workplace problems but instead work smartly to address it.

What salary are you seeking?

I've instructed you to deflect this question and refrain from asking it at other points in the interview process, but eventually they will ask you. There are three different answers you can give for this question.

The first is by stating a salary range, $50,000 to $60,000 for example, and add, "based on my experience, I believe I am on the higher end of this range."

Another option is to push back and say, "We can discuss this once we've both decided that this is a good fit." It puts the onus on them to come up with an appropriate offer.

You can also reply by asking them what the salary range is. This is my most preferred technique as it gives you the most information for proceeding.

Do you have any questions?

Yes! Ask them your intelligent, well-researched questions.

What To Do At The End Of The Interview

As you're concluding the interview, there are some things you should find out. The first question you should ask is very direct, and counterintuitive for some job seekers, but it will help you out tremendously. Ask them: "Do you have any concerns about my ability to do the job?" If they say no, great. If they say yes, they will explain why. If their concern is accurate, you can concede their point but also explain past experiences that highlight your capability. You should also tell them what steps you will take to address their concern if you get the job. For example, you can say that you will take classes or do more research. It's always better to know for sure what you're up against so you can work to address it.

Be sure to thank the interviewer for their time and get the email address of each person you interviewed with. Send out a note to each individual, thanking them for their time and reiterating your enthusiasm for the position. Mention something along the lines that your skills would be a good fit for the position. Keep it brief and to the point.

Before you leave the interview, ask them about the next steps of the hiring process. Find out their hiring timeline. If they eventually hire someone else, still send them a second thank you note for being considered. I know it's difficult to do that when you've been rejected, but it will establish your professionalism. Things can change very quickly and if there's ever another opening at the company, you'll have made an impression with them that will make them more likely to reach out to you again. One of my clients did this and when the person they hired didn't work out, they remembered him and he got the job.

Before you leave, you should ask them for the job. You can always do this by using your 90-second summary. Let them know that this is something that interests you and you would like to proceed to the next round. In your summary, focus on the key things that they are looking for in this position and let them know that these are areas where you excel. You've gone through a lot of preparation to get to this point and are well qualified for the position. If you've told them what you'll do for them, then ask them for the job. A lot of people forget this part but it's important.

Keep all of these points in mind, which I've also listed below. This isn't rocket science, but it is a science, and one you should be very well versed in by now.

- **Ask them if they have any concerns about your ability to do your job**

- **Thank them**

- **Ask about the next steps**

- **Follow up with them**

- **Ask for the job**

Again, if for some reason they offer the position to someone else, don't despair. It's not the end of the world. There is another, better job right around the corner. If you only apply 25% of what I'm teaching you, you will definitely get a job soon.

Summary

This section has given you lots of tools to use during the face-to-face interview process. By using the specific tools I've described, and by doing all of the research and preparation, my clients have reported an interesting thing. Most of them tell me that their interview anxiety has gone way down. They no longer feel that they are at the whim of some inscrutable interviewer, wielding authority over them. They feel empowered by participating in the interview process in a more methodical, well-rehearsed way. When my clients tell me this, I am overjoyed. To get people back to work is fantastic, but to help quell people's anxieties toward the process is icing on the cake. When you interview, keep remembering the following points and you will be amazed by how well your interview goes.

- **Research and prepare for the interview**

- **Practice**

- **Ask and answer questions confidently**

Now that you've learned how to hit the ball out of the park on your interview, it's just a matter of time before someone will want to hire you. When that happens you will need to negotiate a salary. Keep reading for my inside tips on how to handle that.

Discussing Your Job Offer

So you've dazzled them in the interview, and your prospective employer has called you to make an offer. So now what? How do you decide if their terms are fair? How do you avoid selling yourself short? How do you not shoot yourself in the foot? The way you finesse this negotiation is critical to your success in your new position and your long-term career with your employer. If you handle this negotiation well, you will be respected as someone who knows how to take care of him- or herself while still behaving calmly and professionally. If you bungle this negotiation, it could start you off on the wrong foot at your new job and even jeopardize their offer. In this section I will establish some important ground rules that will help you approach your negotiation in a way that will insulate you from some common mistakes job seekers make.

What To Do Before The Negotiation

As with all of the other steps in your job search, knowledge is power. Do your best to find out as much as possible about the company, the position, and the compensation they offer. You will need as many concrete details about the job you're being offered in order to determine what a fair salary is.

Fortunately, the internet has drastically improved the ease with which you'll be able to determine what an appropriate amount is for your job. There are many websites which can let you know how much your salary should be, based on your position, industry, and geographic area. Websites like Payscale.com and Vault.com offer average salaries for thousands of positions. Payscale.com allows people to enter specific information such as geography, experience level, and certifications; or whether the position is with a nonprofit, government agency, small business, or large company to get the most accurate salary data possible.

A negotiating tactic that you must adhere to is never to discuss your previous salary. It has no relevance to your position at this new company. Also, never suggest a salary before they do. Do not bring up salary until they offer you something. If pressed, you can say, "Salary is an important topic. We can discuss it once our mutual interest has been established." Another reply that I've found useful is "if we decide I'm the right person for the job, I'm sure we can agree on a compensation." Another deflection that works is by saying, "At this time, I am more interested in determining if I am the right person for the job." Even though you're not yet discussing an amount, you should know throughout the process what you are worth.

Determine how much you really want and need. Sometimes I have clients who experience "the winners' curse." Yes, they "won" a new job. But unfortunately they agreed to financial terms that leave them struggling just to pay their monthly overhead expenses. Don't negotiate out of fear that the job offer will be taken away. If you receive a job offer, *especially* in this economy, that clearly indicates that you are the best qualified for it and that you did a great job interviewing for and applying for the position. Remember, your interviewer put in a lot of work to find you. The last thing they want to do is go back to filtering through resumes and interviewing candidates. They want *you*. Also, when you negotiate in a respectful manner, you'll demonstrate that you have the business skills they want for someone in that position. Companies actually expect you to negotiate. If you don't they'll be disappointed, since you're hired to be smart. Regardless of your role, they want you to have enough business acumen to negotiate what is best for you. They don't want you to be a pushover.

During the negotiation, you'll also want to get more clarity on what your day-to-day role will be at the company. Even though you asked this during your interview process, it's necessary to reestablish this information as they may have decided to give you a slightly different role after they decided to hire you. Be prepared to have different viewpoints and alternatives to discuss. When you're having the conversation, be sure to cite industry standards that are favorable to your argument. You should also be ready to explain why industry standards that are unfavorable to you do not apply. Don't just have one viewpoint to justify the salary you're negotiating. Have several so you can have a fluid conversation and aren't stopped dead in your tracks if they have a compelling counterargument for one of your ideas.

Practice the negotiation conversation. Do some role-playing and have a friend play the employer. Let them act difficult so you can practice remaining calm. You can always use the mirror too if you can't find anyone to convincingly play your negotiating adversary.

Even though this may be a stressful situation, just remember that companies have a range for each salary and they leave room to move up and down for every position. Do your research and you will have very clear ideas to guide you when you enter this negotiation. Also, remember that you don't need to be someone's bargain. Your prospective employer can see that you will do a lot for the company and that they will get their money's worth.

What To Do During The Negotiation

When you negotiate with your potential employer, remember that *everything* is negotiable: salary, benefits, vacation time, sick time, and any other details. This is an opportunity to refine, communicate and achieve what you want out of your job offer. The key is to act like you're not really negotiating. You must do so in a way that gives the impression that your employer is trying to recruit you. Let them. Tell them what your concerns are. Ask for the things you want without ever suggesting that you won't accept the job if you don't get them. You can use language like, "would it be possible if you could..." or "other companies I've been talking to have offered *x*, *y* and *z*." It will come across like you are not making demands, which is key to the process. You should still be conveying how excited you are about the opportunity and how much you want the job while you are attempting to get the most favorable offer possible.

Negotiating isn't just about salary. Get as much information about what your company tends to give, as there are many different elements of compensation. For some companies, bonuses and equity are the major part of one's offer. For another company, the salary may be the major piece of the pie. Often, particularly early in your career, the best thing you can negotiate is the chance to learn new skills. When you expand your skill set, it will enable you to get a better job and negotiate more money in the future. You can arrange what projects you will be assigned to, who you will be working with, and what sort of training you can receive. This is actually looked upon by employers as a positive quality in their employees. If the company you're working for doesn't offer training or advanced education, it's sometimes possible to get the employer to pay for more classes to advance your skill set.

If you find that you can't negotiate the salary or benefits, you can still negotiate your vacation time or your training opportunities. There are many factors besides salary, so don't just focus on that.

Contrary to the conventional wisdom about "playing it cool" in a negotiation, it's important to show that you're excited about the job offer. Employers like working with someone who's happy to get hired to work for them. Once you've been officially hired, express your gratitude by saying thank you and letting them know how committed you are to the job.

Even if you think you don't want the job, or you're unsure, stay open. Tell them you're excited; you may change your mind. But if you seem indifferent to their job offer, it'll be hard to undo that impression. In fact, an employer may decide to withdraw their offer in favor of hiring someone more enthusiastic.

During the negotiation, effective communication is important, with respect to both talking *and* listening. As they're explaining the salary and all the other parts of the offer, write those details down. After they've fully explained what they're offering you, *then* it's your turn to ask questions. Once they've answered everything, evaluate their offer and go forward with your prepared questions and requests. Once you've done that, it's their turn to counteroffer. Remember, a negotiation is an information exchange that continues until the agreement is reached and the best time to negotiate is *before* you accept a job offer.

Once you are clear about the offer, never accept on the spot. You should ask for some time to think about it. You could say, "based on this information, I would like to think about this and get back to you tomorrow." Or tell them you need to talk it over with your spouse or significant other. Employers are generally okay with this as long as you don't ask for an inordinate amount of time to get back to them. A day or two is usually fine. If it's a Friday, ask to get back to them on Monday.

Sometimes job negotiations can be split up into two meetings. The first meeting could be to discuss the exact particulars of the job and to get clarity on the responsibilities while the second meeting will get into salary and benefits. The key idea is never to make an impulsive decision based on fear and anxiety. This is common, especially for people who have been unemployed for a long time. Do not make an impulsive decision. If they really want you, there is time. So take the time necessary to make the right decision.

Strive for a win-win outcome. Employers, as much as they have their goals and agendas, want to come across as fair because this could possibly be the beginning of a long-term professional relationship. If you have a request, be able to back it up with a reasonable explanation. This is a two-way process. You and your employer are each trying to get something you need in a negotiation. You are both designing the terms so you will be mutually satisfied with the final agreement.

One of my clients, Melanie, was a 26 year old who had just completed her business degree. She was offered an entry-level management position at a company. The salary they offered was less than what the position demanded, which the company rationalized by claiming she was young and inexperienced. Upon my coaching, she was actually able to use her youth to her advantage. She said she was more of an asset to them because she was young, energetic and on the upslope of what would be a long and productive career. She convinced them of her point, that she had a lot to offer, and was able to receive a higher salary. She came away happy, and so did the company after she'd convinced them that she had even more value than they'd previously realized. They got someone who would be with them for the long haul and could put in a lot of years at the organization. You can always use whatever you have to your benefit. If you're older, you can use your experience as a selling point. If you're younger, like Melanie, you can use your youth to your advantage.

But whatever you do, please make yourself very familiar with the points I've addressed in this section. I encourage you to re-read it several times.

The most important ideas you need to retain for your negotiation are:

- **Know that everything is negotiable**

- **Be excited about the job offer**

- **Communicate effectively**

- **Strive for a win-win outcome**

Review

Congratulations on being offered a job! It's proof that you're hirable and have a lot to offer an employer. Just remember that you don't want to haphazardly agree to whatever they offer out of fear. You are in demand, and if you approach this negotiation with a clear head, politeness, and enthusiasm, you will be able to steer this process in way that will be most to your advantage.

Create a "pros" and "cons" list of all the things they have put on the table for you. Everything is negotiable, and your employer expects you to have the wherewithal to be your own advocate in this process. Remember the following points we've discussed before, during and after your negotiation:

- **It's okay to negotiate your job offer.**

- **Plan, prepare and practice before your interview.**

- **Evaluate your job offer.**

I've had clients from all over the world use this process to their advantage in their salary negotiation. As long as you give yourself time to reply to their offer and remember that everything is negotiable, you will probably have the most advantageous salary negotiation you've ever had in your professional life.

Other Creative Ways To Apply For A Job

Job-hunting is an area where creativity always pays off. My more unorthodox clients have impressed me by utilizing some especially creative methods for applying for a job. These innovative tactics are the equivalent of waving a white flag in a sea of red flags. I can't guarantee that you will get hired by using them, but you are certain to get an interview.

There are extreme examples of getting noticed, like the man in Manhattan who wore a sandwich board displaying his resume. Another job seeker, a creative director in advertising, sent advertising agencies boxes of wine with his resume, credits, and contact information on the side. He also hand-delivered these shipments himself by posing as a bike messenger. As I mentioned earlier, Alec Brownstein was a copywriter who broke ground by using Google Adwords to link his ad to searches for CEOs in his field. When those CEOs would "vanity Google" themselves, his ad would pop up and grab their attention.

These are just examples to get you to think in new ways. I'm not necessarily saying they're all right for you, but they are meant to show how freethinking you can be here.

5 Successful Creative Ways To Apply For A Job

Of all the "outside the box" ideas I've heard for applying for a job, there are five that I found the most useful. You don't have to use all five of them. Just using even one would ensure that you stand out from the crowd.

So here are some of my favorite creative methods.

Offer To Work For Free

Offering to work for free on a prospective or probationary basis is one of my all-time favorites. I've successfully used this and have seen it work for my clients as well. However, there are some things you must keep in mind. When you offer to work on a probationary basis, be sure to make clear the length of time you are willing to do so and the reasons why. The length of time should be anywhere from one week to a month, or an amount of time you feel would be sufficient for your employer to judge what you have to offer. This may sound like you're setting yourself up to be exploited, but keep in mind that this never fails to win you at least a trial period. If you are sure of your qualifications, then a trial is all you need. An offer like this indicates how much confidence you have in your ability and value to your employer. Often times, once you are hired, your employer will decide to pay you for your probationary period. You should emphasize to your employer that the reason you're working for free is because you're very passionate about the position and know that you can do an outstanding job for them. Hence, you're willing to back up your claim with no financial risk to your employer. You should also state that you have confidence that you will be taken on as an employee when the trial period is over.

When I used this approach, it was to get my foot in the door at a company that was a leader in my industry. After I'd expressed my willingness to work for free on a trial basis, my employer was so impressed with my dedication that they volunteered to pay me a competitive salary for my 60-day probationary period as well as a signing bonus and a raise when those 60 days were up! Now, you can see why it's one of my favorite methods to use.

Social Media

Twitter Chats

We've already discussed social media as a job-seeking tool, but there are other advanced methods I've seen my clients use. I'd especially like to make the case for using Twitter (www.twitter.com) in your job search. It's a site that brings together millions of people and businesses from all over the world. When people post a comment (or "tweet") on Twitter, they will usually use a hashtag – which is the # symbol - followed by the subject. This is done for ease of searching the site for a specific topic. So if you type #needajob, #jobhuntchat, or #internship, you'll get hundreds of results from people or companies that post their job openings on Twitter, which has become a norm for many companies. You can also search without the hashtag, but hashtag searches will give you the results of people who have specifically geared their post toward a particular subject.

Employer's Facebook And LinkedIn Pages

This item harkens back to what we discussed previously. Joining Facebook groups, especially those set up by an employer you'd like to work for, can help introduce you to a large number of professionals in your industry. Although simply clicking "like" or "join" and calling it a day won't do you much good. You need to interact with other members and post comments that display your interest in the issues affecting your industry. LinkedIn also has groups you can join that offer the same advantages as Facebook groups, such as being able to immediately see a company's job openings.

Facebook Ads, LinkedIn Ads, And Google Ads

My favorite thing about Facebook ads is that you can target who will see your ad by your city, job title, and more. It's a great and relatively inexpensive way to get noticed. With Google ads, you can target by keyword. So as an example, if you're an accountant looking for a job in Los Angeles, you could target with the keywords "accountant looking for a job in Los Angeles." If an employer types in "Los Angeles accountants" your ad will come up.

LinkedIn also has ads, which are similar to Facebook in terms of who you can target. The cost is not prohibitive. You only get charged if someone clicks on your ad. I had a client get a job offer after paying only $6 to Google. Since people won't click on an ad they're not interested in, you'll wind up paying only for the views your ad received. You can also work with the site to restrict how much you will spend per day, and can set the amount to as little as one or two dollars.

LinkedIn Jobs, Facebook Jobs/Apps

LinkedIn jobs is not only highly advanced, but is used by employers around the world. With LinkedIn, you can establish some personal preferences and filters and have a specialized list of job openings emailed to you regularly. Facebook has also started offering more professional networking via its apps like Branch Out, Be Known, and Business Cards. Facebook has an application directory in which you can search its job-hunting apps. The three I mentioned here are the ones I most prefer. Be Known allows users to apply for jobs without leaving Facebook while still maintaining their profile's privacy. With Branch Out, your LinkedIn profile can be imported to create your Branch Out profile. Branch Out also allows you to peruse your friends' professional information if they use the app, and it will show you who is working at a company that has posted a job opening. It's very sophisticated and has many different features. The last app, Business Cards, allows you to create a professional signature similar to an auto-closure on most business emails. You can customize your business card to include your contact information, website, or whatever other information you'd like to have as your virtual signature.

Create A Blog Dedicated To Your Job Search

I've seen this done by some of my clients who enjoy writing. There are numerous free blogging platforms like Wordpress or Tumblr that you can use to create your blog. Tumblr also has a social networking feature so you can import your email, Facebook and Twitter contacts to follow them.

The idea here is to create posts that include your marketing materials such as your complete resume, your cover letter, and your introductory video. You can even ask some of your colleagues who have written you a reference letter to record a recommendation video to post online. Use your blog to link to other content you've created online or other posts that are related to your field. You want to entice people to keep coming back and to tell their online contacts about your blog.

This approach may be time consuming, but it's also very effective. You've provided extensive, detailed information about what you can offer and employees can gather all the pertinent information about you in one place. My clients who have used this were amazed at how quickly the blog yielded them one or more job offers. Almost 100% of my clients got a job instantly when they used this technique.

Make A Video Pitch

The video pitch is something I'm a huge fan of. Your pitch should include all of the reasons why they should hire you, including your experience and education, as well as your statement of what you will do for them. It gets you beyond pen and paper and helps you connect with them. They can see you and your passion and enthusiasm and will be drawn in. I've had clients get hired just from the video.

Have Your Friends Do The Talking For You.

This is similar to your video pitch, except you'll be recording a video of your friends explaining why you're the right person for the job. Your employer will be very impressed by your creativity, innovation, and ability to get people on board with something that (frankly) doesn't personally benefit them.

Give Your Prospective Employer 3 Big Ideas

Giving your employer three big ideas will show them that you are an ideal participant in the company's goals. You can use your three big ideas in your video too. Be sure to include ideas that are big but also achievable, and not just bold for the sake of being bold. Provide examples to substantiate your ideas.

Do you remember the example I gave earlier in the book in which a job seeker wanted to work at a bakery? He compared the prices of what the employer's competitors where charging. He learned that the place where he wanted to work could raise their prices by 10% and still be less expensive than the competition. When he shared with the prospective employer, he was instantly hired at a position above the one he applied for. *This* is the type of big idea that will excite an employer. They'll be amazed that you're giving them great ideas right out of the gate without even being an actual employee. Yet.

Review

Remember, you can do whatever you want, as long as you're being professional and courteous, to stand out. Once you've gotten your employer's attention with your ability to think outside the box, you'll further impress him by demonstrating your knowledge of the company and outlining what you will do for them.

If you use the creative strategies and tactics in this section, you are sure to get at least an interview. Now, if you have tried something that was outside the box and paid off for you, let us hear about it on HelpingFeet.com!

Celebrating Your New Job

I want to talk about an important, but generally overlooked part of the hiring process. Over the past 30 days, you've done a lot of hard work preparing the right application packet; researching the company; readying yourself for your interview; and handling your negotiation with my well-honed strategy. You've negotiated the best job offer in your life, increasing your salary by 10% and giving yourself an extra week of vacation time. You also received a $10,000 sign on bonus. They've asked you to start on Monday, and you have happily agreed. However, you forgot to do one crucial last step of the job getting process. That's to celebrate your new job!

I'm not telling you this just to sound festive. This will actually help you be more relaxed, less stressed out and less nervous on day one of your new job. By "celebrate," I don't just mean a nice dinner, some drinks with your friends or a small shopping splurge. I also want you to take the time to relax and get mentally ready for your new job and your new responsibilities.

I had a personal experience where I learned about the necessity of not skipping this step. When I graduated from school with my MBA, I got a great job offer at Proctor & Gamble that required me to relocate from Denver, Colorado to Cincinnati, Ohio, where the job was. For those of you who don't know, Proctor & Gamble is the number one consumer goods company in the world. This was during the dot com recession in 2002, so I was so excited about my new job that I didn't take time to celebrate or relax. Instead, I immediately packed up and relocated to Ohio to start the new position in a couple of days.

I moved my life so quickly that I'm amazed I didn't get whiplash. I still hadn't even acclimated to the two-hour time difference when I started work. If you recall, I'm not exactly a morning person. My internal clock still hadn't adjusted when I had to wake up for work at 6:30 am, which felt like 4:30. On top of that, I didn't know the city or any people. It was freezing that winter, about 16 degrees Fahrenheit – below freezing - the entire first month I was there. Being in a new city with no friends or family, getting up early every day in freezing cold for the first month was a struggle. After that, I was able to recalibrate and soon excel for the next several years until I relocated to Los Angeles. But that first month was rocky. Now, if I had just taken the time to celebrate and get mentally and physically ready, I would have been much more prepared and had a smoother transition. In hindsight, I wish I'd given myself extra time to go through the following checklist.

Things To Do Before You Start

Before you start your new job, be certain that you have your job offer in writing. If your offer is not in writing, I strongly suggest you not start celebrating until you receive an offer letter, which reflects the terms of your negotiation. I've had clients get verbal offers and never receive a written offer, only to find out later that the employer changed their mind. Some of my clients had already given notice at their current jobs and were put in a very compromising position as a result. So please, no matter how good anything sounds, don't do anything until you receive it in writing. The offer in writing should also include every point you negotiated.

Once you have your written offer, you'll need to get everything in order so you'll be able to rock and roll at your new job on day one. I recommend that you give yourself at least a week before your new job starts. If you're going from one job to another, I advise you to give your two weeks notice, with an extra week between your end date and your start date at your new job. Jumping immediately from one job to another without a break can lead to burnout and a lack of focus at your new job. If possible, I suggest taking your vacation before you start, as you won't be able to take a vacation for a while. It would look really funny if you took a vacation a few months after starting your new job.

During your week (or more) off, give your commute a test drive. You don't want to underestimate the duration of your new drive and show up late on your first day. This is especially necessary if you've relocated for your position. Allow yourself time to familiarize yourself with your new city or state.

It will help yourself tremendously to ask your new boss to send you something that will give you an idea of what your first 30 or 60 days in your new job will be like so that you can get up to speed. You should also ask for an organizational chart for your team, which will help you learn the names, titles and responsibilities of the people you'll be working with. This is especially beneficial if you have difficulty remembering people's names. Showing up knowing who everyone is and what they do will propel you far forward on your learning curve.

Get ready for day one with an eye on creating an impeccable first impression. Show up dressed as best as possible on your first day. For men I recommend a suit, and for women I advise something formal. There will be plenty of time to dress down later. This is not one of those times. Be sure that you're as well groomed as possible, having recently gotten a haircut, manicure, or whatever else you need to look your best. Don't worry about being overdressed. You'll be meeting some of your higher-ups and HR professionals on your first day, so it's important to look professional. At smaller companies, you may even meet with the owner or the CEO. They will also probably take your badge photo, which you'll be looking at for a very long time, so make it a picture you'll want to look at.

So in conclusion, be mindful of these important points:

- **Make sure you have your job offer in writing**

- **Give yourself time to get ready**

- **First impressions matter**

Review

Just remember that getting your offer in writing is vital. Handshake deals are nice, but there's a reason why people put contracts in writing.

Give yourself enough time to relax and recharge. This is for your benefit as well as your new employer's. You may have some nervousness about your new job, especially if you've been out of work for a long time, but remember that they hired you because they see that you can do a lot for them and that you have value. You also have new sales skills, persuasiveness and negotiating abilities that you acquired from this book and demonstrated during your job search. All of that will also serve you in your new job. So again: Congratulations! Now go and celebrate!

Epilogue

I'm honored to have guided you through this process. This thing that I do, and this knowledge that I impart, is more than a career. It feels like a calling to me. I am so grateful to help transform people's lives in this way and I feel lucky to have worked with each of them. I could never have guessed when I started researching this topic so many years ago as a teenager, what it would wind up giving me and so many others. I wish all of you reading this a rewarding career and a long life of happiness and success in whatever you choose to do.

I invite you to join my exclusive Job Getting membership site where you can learn through the video tutorials and interact with other job seekers sharing creative strategies they have used to get jobs. You'll also get job tips and strategies sent to you to help you with your job search.

Here is the link below...

www. helpingfeet.com

Thank you for downloading and reading my book. Please *REVIEW* this book today online and on Amazon.

I need your feedback to make the next version even better. Thank you so much!

Made in the USA
Middletown, DE
25 February 2016